DESIRE/LOVE

Desire/Love

Lauren Berlant

dead letter office

BABEL Working Group

punctum books ✳ brooklyn, ny

Desire/Love
© Lauren Berlant, 2012.

First published in 2012 by
Dead Letter Office, BABEL Working Group
an imprint of punctum books
Brooklyn, New York
punctumbooks.com

The BABEL Working Group is a collective and desiring-assemblage of scholar-gypsies with no leaders, no followers, no top and no bottom, and only a middle. BABEL roams and stalks the ruins of the post-historical university as a multiplicity, a pack, looking for other roaming packs and multiplicities with which to cohabit and build temporary shelters for intellectual vagabonds. We also take in strays.

ISBN-13: 978-0615686875
ISBN-10: 0615686877

Cover image and other images throughout book, unless otherwise noted, from *Imitation of Life* (dir. John Stahl, 1934).

☙

To bossing around and pedagogy; to awkwardness and the supplicant's abjection; to tenderness and surprising discovered depletion; to aggression and passion; to complexity that dreams of simplicity. Our parents are our first examples.

Table of Contents

Desire/Love

Lauren Berlant

PREFACE: DEAR READER

I was assigned to write the entry on "Desire" for the University of Chicago Press volume *Critical Terms for the Study of Gender* in 1998. I read for two years and produced what follows. That volume is only now coming out, in 2013, edited by Gilbert Herdt and Catherine Stimpson. I thank the Press for permission to also publish this entry as a small book.

Meanwhile, punctum books announced a Dead Letter Office imprint, for unpublished work that had been left long in a drawer, and I wondered whether it would be interested in this old thing, this manuscript that, in its first draft, had become two entries, a double entry on Desire and Love — doubled because my practice is always to stage incommensurate approaches to a problem/object in order to attend to its instability, density, and openness. That is the method of what follows within and between the sections. I thank Eileen Joy, Carmen Merport, and Cindy Bateman for helping me so meticulously to see this version through.

I would not spend years of my life writing this book now, and if I were forced to do that, I would not write it this way. There is too much Mommy-Daddy-Me psychoanalysis in relation to other mediations of attachment. There would be many different topics, situations, and much more on the relation of law to lived atmospheres of experience. In addition, the examples would be different. But I have gathered something about love from worrying about the problem of getting exemplification right. The example is *always* the problem for desire/love. The power of any particular case of desire/love has to do with the ways it taps into — embodies or seems to transcend — conscious and unconscious fantasies. Another way to say it: where love and desire are concerned, there are no adequate examples; and all of our objects must bear the burden of exemplifying and failing what drives our attachment to them. I therefore added a bit to the archive but ended up not looking futilely for perfect substitutes. I hope that the concepts generated from the readings will induce new ways to encounter desire/love whether or not you know, identify with, or like the texts with which I am staging conceptual derivations.

Theory, as Gayatri Spivak writes, is at best provisional generalization: I am tracking patterns to enable my readers to see them elsewhere or to not see them, and to invent other explanations. I am interested in lines of continuity and in the ellipsis, with its double meaning of what goes without saying and what has not yet been thought. But, generally, I am still compelled by the descriptions that are here, and from this distance, I am confused to say that, when I read this book, I still learn from it. When it comes to gender and sexuality there are no introductions, even if that is what this book seeks to be. There are only reintroductions, after all, reencounters that produce incitements to loosen, discard, or grasp more tightly to some anchors in the attunement that fantasy offers.

INTRODUCTION

In the study of gender and sexuality, one might expect work on desire and love to be about identity and intimacy, sexual object choice and erotic practice, the disparate dramas lived by various genders, and the centrality of intimate inclinations, emotions, and acts to the assessment of a person's happiness. Ideally such a study would confirm what one already knows about desire and love, as there is nothing more alienating than having one's pleasures disputed by someone with a theory. Yet the ways in which we live sexuality and intimacy have been profoundly shaped by theories — especially psychoanalytic ones, which have helped to place sexuality and desire at the center of the modern story about what a person is and how her history should be read. At the same time, other modes of explanation have been offered by aesthetics, religion, and the fantasies of mass and popular culture, which are not usually realist but often claim to have distilled emotional truths about love's nature and force. In these domains, sexual desire is not deemed the core story of life; it is mixed up with romance, a particular version of the story of love.

♀́

In this essay I engage desire and love in separate entries — the first on desire, the second on love. On the face of it, it makes sense to separate them. Desire describes a state of attachment to something or someone, and the cloud of possibility that is generated by the gap between an object's specificity and the needs and promises projected onto it. This gap produces a number of further convolutions. Desire visits you as an impact from the outside, and yet, inducing an encounter with your affects, makes you feel as though it comes from within you; this means that your objects are not objective, but things and scenes that you have converted into propping up your world, and so what seems objective and autonomous in them is partly what your desire has created and therefore is a mirage, a shaky anchor. Your style of addressing those objects gives shape to the drama with which they allow you to reencounter yourself. By contrast, love is the embracing dream in which desire is reciprocated: rather than being isolating, love provides an image of an expanded self, the normative version of which is the two-as-one intimacy of the couple form. In the idealized image of their relation, desire will lead to love, which will make a world for desire's endurance.

But there is a shadow around this image: who is to say whether a love relation is real or is really something else, a passing fancy or a trick someone plays (on herself, on another) in order to sustain a fantasy? This is a psychological question about the reliability of emotional knowledge, but it is also a political question about the ways norms produce attachments to living through certain fantasies. What does it mean about love that its expressions tend to be so *conventional*, so bound up in institutions like marriage and family, property relations, and stock phrases and plots? This is a question about subjectivity too, therefore, but it is also about ideology. The difficulty of determining love's authenticity has generated a repository of signs, stories, and products dedicated to verifying that the "real thing" exists both among people and in other relations — for example, between people and their nations, their Gods, their objects, or their pets. But these signs of love are not universal, and their conventionality suggests, in addition, that love can be at once genuine and counterfeit, shared and hoarded, apprehensible and enigmatic. Read together, the following entries therefore frame the relation between desire and love as a series of paradoxes that shift according to how the questions about attachment are phrased. Sometimes they refer to people who move within a wide range of genders and sexualities, but often they try to explain structures or conventions of identity and not the sociological or empirical experience of being in desire or having love.

In the first entry, "desire" mainly describes the feeling one person has for something else: it is organized by psychoanalytic accounts of attachment, and tells briefly the recent history of their importance in critical theory and practice. The second entry, on love, begins with an excursion into fantasy, moving away from the parent-child scene of psychoanalysis and looking instead at the centrality to desire of context, environment, or history: it examines ways that the theatrical or scenic structure of fantasy suggests its fundamentally social character, its importance as a site in which a person's relations to history, the present, the future, and herself are performed without necessarily being represented coherently or directly. Whether viewed psychoanalytically, institutionally, or ideologically, love is always deemed an outcome of fantasy. Without fantasy, there would be no attachment and no love. But fantasy will mean many incommensurate things, from unconscious investments in objects of all kinds to dreams inculcated in collective environments. The entry on love describes some workings of romance across personal life and commodity culture, the places where subjects learn to inhabit fantasy in the ordinary course of their actual lives.

We begin with the opening image from the film *Imitation of Life* (dir. John Stahl, 1934). As the introductory credits fade out, the camera cuts to a white bathtub full of water, where a small rubber duck floats. It would be more accurate to say that the duck bobs and weaves, and that it is both fixed in the camera's gaze and unstable in the water. Off camera, we hear a little girl's plaintive voice say: "I want my quack quack!" The child's cry is responded to by what must be a mother's loving disciplinary voice, which replies, "Now, Jessie . . . ." The camera remains all the while fixed on the bobbing duck. As the story develops and bodies become attached to voices, we discover that baby Jessie has a working mother, and that the child is being sent to day care so that the mother can go sell her wares. When the daughter resists being taken there she adopts the language of contract to remind her mother of what love obliges: "I love you and you love me and I don't want to go to the day nursery!" Soon the phone rings, and the mother, Bea Pullman, runs downstairs to answer it, while leaving her child in the bathroom.

On the way to the phone Bea sees that breakfast is burning. She lowers the heat and takes the phone, where she does some business — she sells maple syrup, having taken over her late husband's sales route. Just then an African

American woman comes to the door incorrectly thinking that Bea has advertised for a maid: the woman, Delilah Johnson, is looking for a live-in situation for herself and Peola, her "light-skinned" little girl. Delilah offers Bea her services anyway. Bea resists Delilah's offer, for she has no money to pay wages: at that moment Jessie is overwhelmed by her desire for the "quack quack" and, imagining it within her reach, grabs for it and falls into the bathtub. The white mother runs to save her soaking daughter and the black mother reenters the house, saves the breakfast, and never leaves. The "quack quack" thus rescues them all from their chaotic and impossible domestic scenes.

The white daughter's desire for the duck that bobs and weaves and tempts but which is always out of reach starts the plot that joins the two families' lives: for close to two decades the women and their daughters live together. Marketing a pancake recipe the African American woman provides, they all get wealthy. Yet the white family always takes economic and spatial precedence over its "partner," the black family, and everyone ends up wracked with longing for particular objects which they fail painfully to secure. The world provides neither rest nor freedom for the African American women: the mother desires to "get off her feet" and educate her daughter, but does neither; the daughter wants to be "white, just like I look" and to be free to inhabit any U.S. space, but she too fails to realize that desire. Delilah and Peola, representing the perpetuity of racial, sexual, and economic hardship in the United States, exit the plot before the film finishes. For them, the question of desire can only be answered by transformations in the politically saturated conditions of sustenance the material world does not offer them, changes that cannot be effected by individual will. *Imitation of Life* then closes with the wealthy and beautiful white mother and daughter walking off the screen arm in arm, each secretly longing for a male lover whom they have renounced for each other's sake, while outwardly recalling the film's early moments of desire, chaos, poverty, and plenitude. As the final scene fades out, Bea recalls the day the four women met, saying to her daughter, "and you were saying 'I want my quack quack! I want my quack quack . . .'." It is an extremely bittersweet and defining closing moment, for it turns out that the child's initial utterance of desire prophesies something general about the traumatic destiny of desire in all of their lives.

So what does Jessie really want when she says she wants her "quack quack" — her unavailable working mother, her dead father, or something she senses but cannot name? Is it important that she does not call her toy a duck, but what a duck is said to say, as though what she seeks is something intimate to imitate, something that speaks desiringly to her and that she might come to possess through the exchange of language, and in particular, of being spoken to? Or does it suggest that desire is only secondarily about the relations among bodies, and primarily about voices and the intimate attachments they engender? And what of the daughter's desire for the duck? Would it be overreading to call it erotic? What is the relation between someone's objects of desire and her sexual "identity"? Does it mean something that, later on, Jessie falls in love with a man who studies fish for a living?

And what does the mother mean when she recalls the scene of her daughter's desire? If baby (duck) talk here is the pure language of desire, then perhaps Bea refers, in the end, to the ways one never seems to move beyond the logic of beginnings, of the film's and life's earliest moments. *Imitation of Life* frames these questions in the voice of infantile desire; yet the narrative develops another kind of idiom as well, which tells a story about the sexual, racial, and economic contexts in which African American and white women's fantasies of pleasure and freedom remain just that, intuitions of a world of fulfillment that does not yet exist for them. In any case, in ventriloquizing the plea for the apparitional "quack quack," Jessie's mother captions an entire film's image of pessimism, optimism, language, and desire: the object of desire, which has no proper name, but which in fantasy speaks passionately to you and frames your life, bobs and weaves and hits you more like a boxer than a duck when you reach out to possess it, only to discover that you can never duck in time, but must be dented by it, incidentally, weaving, recovering, and maybe reaching out again for it from within the relation that at once possesses and dispossesses you, forcing you to scavenge for survival while remembering that there is a better beyond to it. The impact of the object, and the impulse that involves the patterning of attachment, are the materials of sexuality and of the optimism (at least for affective relief) that must accompany taking up a position in it. An object gives you optimism, then it rains on your parade — although that is never the end of the story.

Even in its most conventional form, as "love," desire produces paradox. It is a primary relay to individuated social identity, as in coupling, family, reproduction, and other sites of personal history; yet it is also the impulse that most destabilizes people, putting them into plots beyond their control as it joins diverse lives and makes situations. (Thus the painful genre "situation comedy" depends on the association of desire with disaster). Central to the development of narratives that link personal life to larger histories, and to practices and institutions of intimacy, desire also measures fields of difference and distance. It both constructs and collapses distinctions between public and private: it reorganizes worlds.[1] This is one reason why desire is so often represented as political: in bringing people into public or collective life, desire makes scenes where social conventions of power and value play themselves out in plots about obstacles to and opportunities for erotic fulfillment. (Think of *Romeo and Juliet*, *Tristan and Isolde*, *The Scarlet Letter*, *Gone with the Wind*, or *Titanic*.)

The first section of the book will move through analyses of different ways that desire has been zoned by different kinds of human science. I use a language of zoning because desire tends to be associated with specific places.[2] Partly this is to do with how desire materializes in incidents that become events, and sometimes memory. The disturbance desire makes is usually forgettable, and yet even the process of forgetting specifics can transform sites into scenes, spaces laden with affects and feelings that something significant has happened. But the zoning of desire is less

---

[1] See Lauren Berlant, "Intimacy: A Special Issue," *Critical Inquiry* 24 (1998): 281–88, and Lauren Berlant and Michael Warner, "Sex in Public," *Critical Inquiry* 24 (1998): 547–66.

[2] See Berlant and Warner, "Sex in Public."

personal, more normative, too. Consider, for example, erogenous zones, red light districts, master bedrooms, "private parts." Moreover, a relation of desire creates a "space" in which its trajectories and complexities are repeatedly experienced and represented; and as its movement creates tracks that we can follow on "the body" and in "the world," it creates an urge for mapping.

Both the theories and the profession of psychoanalysis have been crucial to the development of desire's modern conventions and forms — at least in the United States and Europe. A psychoanalytic model that locates the truth of a person in sexuality has been central to many of the modern narratives and norms that organize personal and institutional life. In addition, during the twentieth century in the U.S. a more general therapeutic or "self-help" culture has developed, in which it is presumed that individuals both can and need to fix themselves. An industry of mental health experts has flourished, focusing largely on a range of individual problems with intimacy: sexuality, family, and love are the main sites of stress and pedagogies of self-care, while concerns about food, alcohol, drug, or money addictions conventionally appear as symptoms of a person's damaged self or self-esteem. Many people now learn to believe or hope that they can purchase access to this expertise about surviving the destabilizing effects of desire, either by going into therapy or purchasing a variety of commodities such as books, diet foods, and over-the-counter medications, all means to supposedly enable "mental health" and/or happiness. Talk shows, advice columns, and even state agencies argue that solving problems with love and desire is the individual's responsibility.

In contrast, this essay presumes that individuation is a historical process through which people are constructed or made specific, and through which persons learn to identify particular aspects of themselves as their core traits. "Identity" might be defined as the kind of singularity that an individual is said to have: paradoxically, identity is also the individual's point of intersection with membership in particular populations or collectivities. Traditional psychoanalysis is a liberal discourse, in that its recourse to the individual requires a model of the abstract, universal, or structurally determined individual, who is inevitably organized and disorganized in a certain way by the encounter with desire. This presumption about structuration becomes too often attached to an image of happy normal individuals who adhere to measures of propriety in a prevailing social world. (Gilles Deleuze, from a different angle, calls this subject of data a "dividual," to emphasize that individuality itself is a cluster of qualities that don't express the totality of a person but rather her value as data to the reproduction of the normative world.)[3] Thus, when we think about desire we will not think as much about the optimism and promise it usually expresses. Instead, we will think about sexuality as a structure of self-encounter and encounter with the world; about modern ideologies and institutions of intimacy that have installed sexuality as the truth of what a person is; that promote a narrowed version of heterosexuality as a proper cultural norm, and regulate deviations from it; and that none-theless yield some carefully demarcated space to some kinds of non-normative sexuality, such as gay and lesbian. We will then engage the ideologies of love marketed by the entertain-ment industries of western mass culture, and ask how love became a way of imagining particular utopias of gender and sex. Through-out we will be thinking about gender, identity, and desire, both as abstractions and as materialized in history: we will also be reflecting on kinds of longing that are not "normal" in that they are not confined to or well-described by any sexual identity form.

One more thing: as the tempting and elusive floating duck shows us, there is no way definitively to capture desire, in an object or in theory. This is why critical thought about what

---

[3] Gilles Deleuze, "Postscript on the Societies of Con-trol," *October* 59 (1992): 3–7.

desire is almost inevitably becomes theoretical thought about thought itself: the minute an object comes under analytic scrutiny, it bobs and weaves, becomes unstable, mysterious, and recalcitrant, seeming more like a fantasy than the palpable object it had seemed to be when the thinker/lover first risked engagement. So, in order to explain some things about desire and love, this small book will not even attempt to claim to understand their essential structure. Thinking about relations of desire and love as intensified zones of attachment, I will try to give you ways to identify their activity, track their movement, and map out the dents, incidents, accidents, and patterns of event they make on people and the world in which they circulate.

DESIRE

Psychoanalysts do not agree on what the idea or
entity "desire" is: conventionally associated
with romantic concepts like love or lust, desire
is also associated with the Freudian categories
of "drive" and "libido," which refer to a flow of
sexual energy that is said to put pressure on the
individual (or "subject," someone with subjectivity) to move from sensual autonomy to a
relation with the world. In this model, "desire"
articulates the drives, or the infantile excitation
that operates throughout the subject's life, with
relation to objects: primary objects in the
original caretaking environment, like the breast
or the mother, and secondary ones through
which the subject can repeat the experience of
desiring in her adult life. In contrast, a Lacanian
model would call desire less a drive that is
organized by objects and more a drive that
moves beyond its objects, always operating with
them and in excess to them, with aims both to

preserve and destroy them. Different psycho-analytic schools offer many motives for this doubleness, all of which have to do with the inevitability of ambivalence, to which we shall later return.

These points about desire are crucial: desire is memorable only when it reaches toward something to which it can attach itself; and the scene of this aspiration must be in a relation of repetition to another scene. Repetition is what enables you to recognize, even unconsciously, your desire as a quality of yours. Desire's formalism — its drive to be embodied and reiterated — opens it up to anxiety, fantasy, and discipline.

It is important at this juncture, however, to distinguish between some kinds of anxiety and others. "Normal" pathways of desire expose people to different risks than do non-normative desires (note the awkward writing: in most thesauruses, there are no eloquent value-neutral terms for the non-normative. It is designated by words associated with the immoral or the monstrous). Heterosexual desire takes place in heteronormative culture — that is, a site where heterosexuality is presumed not only to be a kind of sexuality, but the right and proper kind. For all of the instability, incoherence, and vulnerability heterosexuality engenders in the subjects who identify with it, the context in which it takes place not only supports it morally and organizes state, medical, educational, and commodity resources around it, but considers it the generic (the default, the natural) form of sexuality itself. An extraordinary amount of discipline, scrutiny, and threat keeps many heterosexuals behaving according to "the straight and narrow," but these institutional forces are also distributed in everyday life through informal policing — aggressive commentary, passive aggressive judgmental murmuring asides and glances, and jokes, for example.

In contrast, gay, lesbian, transgendered and even less-standard sexualities have few generalized spaces or institutions of support; nowhere are they the taken-for-granted of the word "sexuality." This means that along with experiencing the vulnerability that comes to anyone who takes the risk of desiring the pleasures of intimacy, they bear the burden of experiencing a general devaluation of their desires, which are generally considered anti-thetical to the project of social reproduction. Gays and lesbians, for example, are constantly exposed to a whole range of unpleasant consequences — from fear of familial rejection and social isolation to underemployment and physical brutality, simply because of their sexual identity. To the phobic — those who fear instabilities of privilege and embrace the social as a site of sameness, non-normative sexualities threaten fantasies of the good life that are anchored to images of racial, religious, class, and national mono-culture. This is why developing *spaces* of relative gay and lesbian saturation has been so important to building a less homophobic world: otherwise, non-normative sexualities have, during the twentieth century, mainly represented negative forms of social value, establishing a boundary through taboo and terror that has helped to prop up heterosexual culture so successfully that people are frequently surprised by their own normativity.[4] Moreover, if by the time you read this, LGBTQ couples are an ordinary event in the everyday, this does not mean that heteronormativity has been vanquished. It might mean that one of its qualities — the couple or the family form, for example — is ruling the moral, legal, economic, and/or social roost in such a way that other-oriented practices might

---

[4] See George Chauncey, *Gay New York: Gender, Urban Culture, and the Makings of the Gay Male World, 1890-1940* (New York: Basic Books, 1994); John D'Emilio and Estelle B. Freedman, *Intimate Matters: A History of Sexuality in America* (New York: Harper and Row, 1988); Elizabeth Lapovsky Kennedy and Madeline Davis, *Boots of Leather, Slippers of Gold: The History of a Lesbian Community* (New York: Routledge, 1993); Esther Newton, *Cherry Grove Fire Island: Sixty Years in America's First Gay and Lesbian Town* (Boston: Beacon Press, 1993); and Michael Warner, *Fear of a Queer Planet: Queer Politics and Social Theory* (Minneapolis: University of Minnesota Press, 1993).

be held in contempt and/or illegalized. It might not, though! The incoherent relation of privileged fear and deference (within the ordinariness of social proximity) remains one of the great challenges to political and social analysis.

Freudian psychoanalytic theory popularized and drastically transformed how normative and non-normative sexuality and sexual desires were being conceptualized and experienced at the beginning of the twentieth century. It would be imprudent to try here to summarize all of Freud's work on these subjects.[5] What follows are some of the ways Freud thought about the *forms* desire takes. Questions about the designs of desire not only have consequences for the ways we think about intimate sexual practices, sexual identity, identification, and attachment: they also help us track sexuality in the political sphere and mass

---

[5] For a start, see Teresa Brennan, *The Interpretation of the Flesh: Freud and Femininity* (New York: Routledge, 1992); Jean Laplanche and Jean-Bertrand Pontalis, *The Language of Psychoanalysis*, trans. Donald Nicholson-Smith (London: Hogarth Press, 1973); Rosalind Minsky, ed., *Psychoanalysis and Gender: An Introductory Reader* (New York: Routledge, 1996); and Jacqueline Rose, "Introduction II," in *Feminine Sexuality: Jacques Lacan and the Ècole Freudienne*, eds. Jacqueline Rose and Juliet Mitchell (New York: W.W. Norton, 1982), 27–57.

entertainment, since these public sites help to designate which forms of desire can be taken for granted as legitimate, in contrast to those modes of desiring that seem to deserve pity, fear, and antagonism.

It may seem far away from these social issues to turn to infantile sexuality, but it is here that psychoanalysis has historically developed its ways of describing the "normal" forms of activity, identification, and object-choice that organize the subject's primary experiences of pleasure, trauma, and desire. Right away we see that Freud's model not only revolutionized sexuality by locating the developmental origins of adult sexual practice in the acts and wishes of infants and children, but also that it produced an idea of eros far more complex and ambivalent than that which we find in popular notions of the Oedipal complex and romance ideology. These versions of love tend to disavow erotic ambivalence and install, in its place, a love plot — a temporal sequence in which erotic antagonism or anxiety is overcome by events that lead to fulfillment.[6]But

---

[6] See Tania Modleski, *Loving with a Vengeance: Mass-Produced Fantasies for Women* (Hamden, CT: Archon Books, 1982); Leslie W. Rabine, "Romance in the Age of Electronics: Harlequin Enterprises," in *Feminist Criticism and Social Change: Sex, Class and Race in Literature and Culture*, eds. Judith Newton and Deborah Rosenfelt (New York: Methuen, 1985),

in Freud's model the confirming and caring economy of love, involving both giving and receiving on the model of maternal plenitude, is all bound up with an economy of aggression. In this model, to love an object is to attempt to master it, to seek to destroy its alterity or Otherness. Here, aggression is not the opposite of love, but integral to it: one way to think about this is that in love, the lover hungers to have her object *right where she can love it*. This is why sadism, masochism, and perversion are not exceptions to the rule of desire in Freud's model, but integral to human attachment. Love enables the pressure of desire's aggression to be discharged within a frame of propriety. In this view Freud is supported by other schools of psychoanalytic thought that, for all their differences, agree that the will to destroy (the death drive) and preserve (the pleasure principle) the desired object are two sides of the same process.[7] Some post-Freudians, however,

---

249–67; Janice A. Radway, *Reading the Romance: Women, Patriarchy, and Popular Literature* (Chapel Hill: University of North Carolina Press, 1984); Jean Saunders, *The Craft of Writing Romance* (London: Allison and Busby, 1995); and Sharon Thompson, *Going All the Way: Teenage Girls' Tales of Sex, Romance, and Pregnancy* (New York: Hill and Wang, 1995).

[7] For example, see Melanie Klein and Joan Rivière, *Love, Hate, and Reparation* (New York: Norton,

argue that Freud's model produces an image of sexuality as fundamentally masochistic.[8] This is because, regardless of how it is experienced by the desiring subject, desire can overwhelm thought, shatter intention, violate principles, and perturb identity. It is as though desire were a law of disturbance unto itself to which the subject must submit to become a subject of her own unbecoming.

There are intense debates in the psychoanalytic literature as to whether the primary form of infantile desire is *allosexual* (directed

---

1964); D.W. Winnicott, *Collected Papers: Through Paediatrics to Psychoanalysis* (London: Hogarth, 1958); D.W. Winnicott, *Playing and Reality* (London: Routledge, 1971); and D.W. Winnicott, *Home is Where We Start From: Essays by a Psychoanalyist* (New York: Norton, 1986).

[8] See Leo Bersani, *The Freudian Body: Psychoanalysis and Art* (New York: Columbia University Press, 1986); Teresa de Lauretis, *The Practice of Love: Lesbian Sexuality and Perverse Desire* (Bloomington: Indiana University Press, 1994); Sigmund Freud, *Three Essays on the Theory of Sexuality*, in *The Standard Edition of the Complete Psychological Works of Sigmund Freud*, trans. and ed. James Strachey, vol. 7 (1905; London: Hogarth Press, 1949), 158–59); and Sigmund Freud, "The Economic Problem of Masochism," in *The Standard Edition of the Complete Psychological Works of Sigmund Freud,* trans. and ed. James Strachey, vol. 12 (1924; London: Hogarth Press, 1957).

toward the other — in this case, the mother, the source of nourishment, her breast, her milk) or *auto-erotic*.[9] But without boundaries or the capacity to resist stimuli (the function of the ego, which the infant does not yet have), the infant might also be said to be unable to distinguish between her own body as erotogenic zone and the nourishment that seems to be organized around her bodily need.

At first the erotogenic zones are not organized genitally: the infant's whole body, the skin, and diffuse feelings of contact and movement provide the ongoing experience of pleasure. This is "polymorphous perversity." At the same time the infant's body is in a relation of exchange with its caretaking environment, and the sensuality of that environment begins to produce excitation on the infant's body, with its pulsating zones of repeated need, stimulation, and gratification. At some point the infant realizes that she is not continuous with the caretaking environment/mother/breast that she relies on for nurturance and pleasure. The infant's recognition of separateness produces a primary trauma, and it is the site at which reactive aggression and love become entwined in desiring activity. At this point,

---

[9] I derive this usage of allo- and auto- from Eve Kosofsky Sedgwick, *Epistemology of the Closet* (Berkeley: University of California Press, 1990), 59.

Jean Laplanche argues, the child develops strategies of auto-eroticism, which is the only site of certain satisfaction once the mother is perceived to be Other. The infant also re-routes her self-pleasure back into the world, seeking substitutes for the lost breast / mother so that, as Freud writes, "The finding of an object [of desire] is in fact a re-finding of it." But the infant (as child and adult) soon sees that even the gratifications of this re-finding are mixed with anxiety, doubt, and disappointment, for the substitute object of desire is always more and less than the lost real thing.[10]

The infant becomes motivated to sociability by her drive to reclaim an impossible attachment. She learns to give love as care, as manipulation, and as violence in order to get it. This is also the moment at which memory fragments of unfulfilled wishes generate the materials of the unconscious: the unconscious is caused by the repression of these traumas and wishes, which are later to become represented in symptoms, patterns, reiterations, and other forms that mark the

---

[10] Freud, *Three Essays on the Theory of Sexuality*, 222. See also Jean Laplanche, *Life and Death in Psychoanalysis*, trans. Jeffrey Mehlman (Baltimore: Johns Hopkins University Press, 1976), 17–21.

half-remembered experience of lost love.[11] *From this point of view, traumatic loss of continuity with the world is the core motive for the formation of subjectivity.* Freud's concept of melancholia might usefully clarify this: the melancholic is one who incorporates a lost object of desire into her ego, so that she never fully experiences the loss, since the loved one, even in absence, becomes merged with the self. This confusion of presence and absence leads to other-directed sadness and anger (I love them, why did they leave me, I am not myself without them, they cannot leave me) and to self-directed anger (I must not be worthy of love). After the traumatic separation from the mother, it is said, melancholia becomes integral to love itself, a form of masochism derived from the simultaneity of self-loss and the loss of the loved one. [12] Melancholia mirrors inversely the idealizing narratives about merged souls more happily associated with love. Indeed, Freud speculated that one's primary love affair is with one's ego, projected out onto the world and returned as difference. His complaint about

---

[11] See Hélène Cixous, "Portrait of Dora" [1976], trans. Sarah Burd, *Diacritics* 13.1 (1983): 32 [2–32], and Adam Phillips, "Freud and the Uses of Forgetting," in *On Flirtation: Psychoanalytic Essays on the Uncommitted Life* (London: Faber and Faber, 1994), 22–38.

[12] See Bersani, *The Freudian Body*, 81–96.

homosexuality and hysterical femininity was that they were forms of narcissism without the necessary mediation of corporeal difference, and thus perhaps without the proper relation to primary trauma. Later in his career, the pervasiveness of homosexual desires in his patients returned to destabilize his early taxonomies.

On discovering her specific difference from the nurturing environment, the infant begins to construct forms that reproduce the predictable world of repeated affect she initially experienced. This is the value of Oedipal triangulation. Freud also holds that the child's entry into Oedipal relations has other, more developmental, functions: it secures the subject's sexual object-choice, organizes genitality in its proper sequence, and enables the formation of the super-ego, about which more below. At this stage Freud takes his model of desire from heterosexual masculinity. He describes a double process of attachment for the child: object-love between the child and his mother and identification between the child and his father. *Identification* with the same-sex parent is considered *metaphoric*, as a narcissistic relation of likeness produces a new sense of bodily continuity for the child; in contrast, the child's love for the mother now develops through the logic of difference Freud calls *object-choice*, a *metonymic* relation that involves substituting like objects for the originary relation of plenitude — an adult desire for women's breasts, for example, substitutes for the infant's desire for milk. At the same time this relation is also called an *anaclitic* or *propping* relation, as the child's desire is structured by proximity, a relation of intimate difference, and a longing to overcome distance.

The Oedipal crisis occurs when the child realizes that, like all economies, the Oedipal economy involves scarcity: the father is his rival for the mother's love. Freud posits that each subject experiences a positive and a negative Oedipal process, the sexual ambivalence of which expresses the fundamental bisexuality of humans. The boy wants to vanquish the father; at the same time, because he identifies with the father, the son also develops a masochistic relation to his own aggression, develops a virtually "feminine" attitude to protect his rival, and projects his own hostility onto the mother who then figures as a threat to both men.[13] But for "normal" masculine identity to develop, the Oedipal crisis must be resolved by an intensified identification with the father. Freud

---

[13] See Sigmund Freud, "The Ego and the Id," in *The Standard Edition of the Complete Psychological Works of Sigmund Freud*, trans. and ed. James Strachey, vol. 19 (1923; London: Hogarth Press, 1961), 32–33, and Gilles Deleuze, *Masochism: An Interpretation of Coldness and Cruelty*, trans. Jean McNeil (New York: George Brazilier, 1971).

argues that this resolution is achieved by the boy's discovery of sexual difference — the shock of the mother's vagina, read as a traumatized site of penile "castration" — which has both catastrophic and productive effects on the boy.

One "healthy" effect of the discovery that the mother is castrated is the smashing of the Oedipus complex.[14] This development seems to resolve many sites and structures of shame in heterosexual development, not the least of which is the incest taboo. This enables the boy to desire as his father desires without hurting the father, because the son's desire now travels beyond the mother and outside of the family. From this develops the super-ego or ego-ideal, which tries to protect the boy from future trauma by disciplining his desire toward proper objects. Along with guaranteeing his heterosexual masculinity, this solution protects his primary relation to his mother: she remains the beloved original source of care and nourishment, but her frightening sexual difference requires that she be replaced by other women. Sexual attachments to new

---

[14] Sigmund Freud, "Some Psychical Consequences of the Anatomical Distinction Between the Sexes," in *The Standard Edition of the Complete Psychological Works of Sigmund* Freud, trans. and ed. James Strachey, vol. 19 (1925; London: Hogarth Press, 1961), 256–57.

women provide an opportunity for the boy to perform successful masculinity by overcoming the now doubly post-traumatic ambivalence he has toward his mother (originating at the breast and the vagina).

Castration anxiety results in the more intensified homosocial identification that also constitutes normative masculinity. If one admits this speculative perspective, boys identify with the father and with men generally not only because they are the same gender: they develop solidarity because they have faced the same threats, and feel the same strangeness of anxiety and ambivalence at the scene of their attachment to desire for women.

But sometimes the trauma of castration anxiety paralyzes the subject, freezing his sexuality at the point of crisis itself and endangering his successful accession to ordinary hetero-masculinity. This is when perversions like *fetishism* develop. Freud's essays "Fetishism" and "Medusa's Head" suggest that the crisis of phallic fragility that binds men to each other and produces a polarized set of fascinations with women's bodily difference — aggressive/abject, idealized/disgusted — can also produce a formalism that repairs anxiety by covering it over, thus enabling the male to disavow his activated ambivalence toward women. The fetish is such a form.

A fetish is an erotically endowed object that someone can possess and control, yet, paradoxically, the fetish seems to control or possess the person who thinks she possesses it. It turns a story of masculine desire for women into a story of victimization by women that ends up in a scenario of heroic repair. Fetishism is fundamentally an aesthetic crisis: just as the Medusa petrifies whoever looks at her face, the boy, shocked at his mother's genital difference from him, displays his realization on his body. He becomes stiff (as in scared and as in erect); he visualizes pubic hair teeming with snakes (or penises) in the hair on his mother's head. In other words, the boy's body and sensorium produce representations of the mother's lost, castrated penis: the fetish is that which represents the object, its presence, and its absence. Its magic is that it protects the boy from experiencing absolute loss. Frequently, it is something the boy associates with the floor beneath his mother's dress or other surfaces associated with her (shoes, embroidery, fur). As such, the fetish enables desire to be controlled, to be manageable, to be comprehended, signified, and also screened out by the material form. Moreover, the fetish has no uniqueness nor singularity, like the penis; it can always be possessed, reproduced, replaced, and collected. Thus it encompasses value and valuelessness, and construes desire through aggression and protectiveness. But the contradictions and complexities that motivate fetishism are hidden by the fetishized object. If the fetish originally marks a traumatic event, its availability for reproduction separates it from the event, de-contextualizes it into pure form, and enables the fetishist to become absorbed in an abstract present tense marked by repetition, fascination, and analytic distraction.

The sublimation of sexual desire into objects that replace the original one(s) also, para-doxically, protects the original object, by pro-tecting the child's attachment from any future destabilization. Indeed, in Freud's essays on the psychology of love, he suggests that men who have not successfully worked through Oedipal trauma will produce adult object choices that tend either toward overvaluation of the loved object or denigration of a series of inadequate women. (These are the two sides of fetishism in his analysis.) Here, as elsewhere, he suggests that antithetical relations of desire, like that of idealization and revulsion, can actually formally figure the same motive for desire's circulation. Frequently, he suggests that the fundamental ambivalence, bisexuality, and/or incoherence of human drives motivate the formalism of desire: but, he says, "civilization" requires their disavowal and sublimation to the good of heterosexual nor-malcy. Freud writes, "The final outcome of sexual development lies in what is known as the normal sexual life of the adult, in which the pursuit of pleasure comes under the sway of the reproductive function and in which the component instincts, under the primacy of a single erotogenic zone, form a firm organization directed towards a sexual aim attached to some extraneous sexual object."[15] To the extent that this "extraneous sexual object" enables the desiring subject to deny his ambivalence on behalf of attaining sexual and intimate normalcy, his desire is fetishistic: that is, the fetish reproduces the general structure of desire, which is an activity that aims at repeating pleasure by finding substitutes for a lost or unstable object.

Freud's account of the accession of girls to heterosexual femininity through "reverse" Oedipalization has all the quality of a bad copy: sometimes he argues that the process is simply transposed, such that the girl's identification with her mother and object-cathexis on her father come into crisis with the same conjoining of aggression and masochism as he finds in boys. He also argues that girls are not as motivated as boys to move through Oedipalization to discipline by the super-ego because girls are always already castrated, and thus unprovoked by its threat. This suggests to Freud that women therefore develop weaker super-egos, a weaker sense of justice, a more

---

[15] Freud, *Three Essays on the Theory of Sexuality*, 197.

contingent sense of self, and more easily dis-organized and pathological desires.

Yet Freud wrote many things during his career that do not quite cohere. On the subject of female masochism, for example, he offers a political analysis as well. He argues that women do possess a stream of threat-induced erotic aggressivity — just less intensively so than men — but that there is no socially sanctioned place for it, no drama in which female aggression accrues social value.[16] Since desire always finds an object through which it can sustain itself, even at the cost of massive misrecognition, that aggression will then tend to return to its origin, the woman. This social explanation of "female masochism" contradicts the kinship-centric one we have been tracing, and marks an internal tension in Freud's work that continues in contemporary psychoanalysis. This incoherence does not necessarily delegitimate psycho-analysis as such: it typifies a general problem that characterizes thought about power and subjectivity in modern capitalist contexts, in which "the individual" tends to be seen paradoxically, as a being driven by appetites

---

[16] See Sigmund Freud, "Femininity," in *New Introductory Essays on Psychoanalysis*, in *The Complete Psychological Works of Sigmund Freud*, trans. and ed. James Strachey, Vol. 22 (1933; London: Hogarth Press, 1964), 132–35.

and structures induced by the world and
as a sovereign, autonomous force relative
to the constantly changing institutions of
social life. But psychoanalysis also has shown
that one's own incoherence-in-ambivalence
meets up with the incoherence of social aims
and demands in ways that either mirror each
other or induce multiple fantasies of relief
and repair. It has been suggested that the
lack of fit is an un-bridgeable space or
aporia covered over by *ideology*, which so
successfully produces subjects who see the world
from the perspective of their own individual
stories that other more structural explanations of subjectivity seem themselves to
violate the specificity and uniqueness of
each individual's identity in the world.[17]
Critical theory's engagement with desire has
also mobilized words like "excess," to refuse the
"sense" that ideology makes out of explanations that do not cohere with an indi-
vidualist model of sovereign desire, and
which potentially enables more mutually structured transformations of subjects and worlds.

Needless to say, there has been much critical
feminist work focusing on the male benefit of
concepts like penis envy and feminine lack that

---

[17] See Slavoj Žižek, "The Spectre of Ideology," in
Mapping Ideology, ed. Slavoj Žižek (London: Verso,
1994), 21 [1–33] and *The Sublime Object of Ideology*
(London: Verso, 1989).

organize much of what Freud has to say about women's desire. But does this mean that Freud has no knowledge, after all, about what women want? Are his fictions of psychic order mainly symptoms of a more general turn-of-the-century misogynist malaise or a generically patriarchal imaginary? This position has been strenuously argued. But Freud's intuitions have also been remade into positive values by analysts like Nancy Chodorow, who suggest that women's identification with mothers makes women more flexible and less violent than men, rather than weaker or more masochistic. Jessica Benjamin, in contrast, argues that Freud's highly negative account of Otherness (traditionally the place of the Mother, the feminine) is both right and sadly lacking. Following Donald Winnicott, she argues that the fundamental ambivalence of desiring subjects toward their "objects" is just that, ambivalence: if one aspect of the subject's response to the violence of her originary traumatic separation is the experience of the enigmatic Otherness of the lover, the desiring subject nonetheless retains a desire to recognize her intimate as a person, a unique self. For even if, when someone desires, one motive is the mastery of the desired Other, it is also the case that people seek to recognize the Other as a subject, for only under these conditions can humans truly receive the recognition they crave. Benjamin's model of desire is, at root, far less organized by the antinomies of sexual difference than psychoanalytic models tend to be. Finally, Jacqueline Rose argues that Freud's work powerfully shows that sexual difference (heterosexualized gender identity) never achieves purity or stability. It always produces anxiety and lapses into incoherence. Or, as Freud himself contends, "pure masculinity and femininity remain uncertain theoretical constructions of uncertain content."[18] No powerful umbrella theory has been invented to resolve these different readings of gender, sexuality, and desire in psychoanalysis.[19]

One imputed result of women's weaker erotic organization — that is, not having displaced and condensed the traumatized love of the mother onto a fragile and over-symbolized body part — is that women are deemed incapable of fetishism. Since fetishism has been shown to be a central structure of "normal" sexuality, women's lack of relation to it in traditional psychoanalysis has contributed to the sense that women are hysterical or

---

[18] Freud, "Some Psychical Consequences," 258.

[19] See Nancy Chodorow, *The Reproduction of Mothering: Psychoanalysis and the Sociology of Gender* (Berkeley: University of California Press, 1978), Jessica Benjamin, *Like Subjects, Love Objects: Essays on Recognition and Sexual Difference* (New Haven: Yale University Press, 1995), and Jacqueline Rose, *Sexuality in the Field of Vision* (London: Verso, 1986).

narcissistically disordered with respect to the objects they desire. Teresa de Lauretis, Naomi Schor, Emily Apter, and others counter this implication. Schor argues that there is a feminine fetishism, and that it recognizes the play of presence and absence, aggression and idealization, trauma and plenitude between the lover and the loved in the classic model of fetishistic desire: but because women's "castration" is a given, women can have an ironic relation to their erotic repetitions: they can admit them without disavowing or doing violence to them.[20]

De Lauretis argues, instead, that there is a specificity to lesbian fetishism. If the fetish marks the traumatic loss of bodily totality for the lover who projects it onto the beloved's negatively valued corporeal difference, then lesbian desire has to create its own aesthetic markers of desired and threatening "difference," because the distinctions between female lovers cannot be mapped onto sexually "different" bodies. Therefore castration, she

---

[20] See Naomi Schor, "Female Fetishism: The Case of Georges Sand," *Poetics Today* 6 (1985): 301–10; "Fetishism and Its Ironies," in *Fetishism as Cultural Discourse: Gender, Commodity, and Vision*, ed. Emily Apter and William Pietz (Ithaca: Cornell University Press, 1993), 92–100; and *Reading in Detail: Aesthetics and the Feminine* (New York: Methuen, 1987).

argues, is irrelevant to lesbians. As a result, inter-subjective fantasy plays a bigger part in the production of lesbian love. In contrast to Freudian and heterosexual feminist theories of desire — which see love primarily as a fetishistic fantasy that obscures the very object of desire who animates it — de Lauretis's version of lesbian fetishism requires two lovers who fantasize together.[21] The erotic aesthetic they generate produces an intimate boundary, a space of bodily distinction and difference, that their desire crosses and recrosses — but not in order to destroy or make order from desire's unstable process. For de Lauretis the fetishistic "perversion" of lesbian desire is productive, not destructive, of love.

We have been tracking the relation between Freudian theories of infantile desire and their post-traumatic repetition in adult life. We have seen, so far, that, even if the libido is ungendered, each gender is associated with particular forms of representing and processing the ambivalent pressures of the drive's energy, whether generated by bisexuality, or traumas of infantile separation and castration. We have also seen that idealization, aggression, and

---

[21] De Lauretis, *The Practice of Love*, 228–86.

melancholia, as well as "perversions" like masochism and fetishism, seem integral to the ordinary career of desire, as it struggles and fails continuously to find ideal objects on which it can rest. The formalism of desire thus both produces perversion and manifests itself in narratives that aim toward normalcy but, para-doxically, never reach completion: even "nor-mal" desire operates incrementally, restlessly testing out its objects.[22]

This might seem a melancholy conclusion, especially if your dream of desire is sustained by a particular combination of pleasure and satis-faction. Yet, as Eve Sedgwick argues, even if desire fails to find objects adequate to its aim, its errors can still produce pleasure: desire's fundamental ruthlessness is a source of creativity that produces new optimism, new narratives of possibility, even erotic experi-mentality.[23] Most people, however, do not experience consciously the benefits of the vicissitudes of their desires. This is in part because they frequently confuse their desire for the comfort and self-development of a reliable

---

[22] See Bersani, *The Freudian Body*, 63–64, and Kaja Silverman, *The Acoustic Mirror: The Female Voice in Psychoanalysis and Cinema* (Bloomington: Indiana University Press, 1988), 1–41.

[23] Eve Kosofsky Sedgwick, "A Poem is Being Written," in *Tendencies* (Durham: Duke University Press, 1993), 206–11.

love with a desire for a degree of stability and non-ambivalence that live intimacy can rarely sustain. Additionally, people are schooled to recognize as worthwhile only those desires that take shape within the institutions and narratives that bolster convention and traditions of propriety. They learn, further, to be afraid of the consequences when their desire attaches to too many objects or to objects deemed "bad": whether they find themselves longing for persons of an illegitimate or merely inconvenient-to-comfort sexuality, race, class, ethnicity, or religion, or marital status.

Thus even though the shapes desire takes can be infinite, one plot dominates scenes of proper fantasy and expectation. It is a plot in which the patterns of infantile desire develop into a love plot that will be sutured by the institutions of intimacy and the fantasy of familial continuity that links historical pasts to futures through kinship chains worked out in smooth ongoing relations. In the U.S., this plot has been legally and aesthetically privileged, although it has been widely adapted: and as a dream of what life should provide the desire for conventional love remains fairly strong across many fields of social difference. We have already seen that the public world of fixed gender identities organized by heterosexuality relies on the successful propagation of the belief that "normal" sexuality and desire are not only possible, but imaginable, natural, and right. We have also seen that, for single or nonreproductive heterosexuals and for gays, lesbians, bisexuals, and transgendered subjects, the costs of not acceding to normatively sexualized life narratives are both ordinary and extreme, from shame to corporeal punishment by the carceral state and its citizens.

§ PSYCHOANALYSIS, SEX, AND REVOLUTION

The world of conventional intimate behavior came under vigorous attack during the radical upheavals of the 1960s: indeed, we would not be studying the category "desire" today had it not been a keyword in the anti-institutional political struggles of that period. The uses to which the category "desire" was put by European and U.S. social radicals in and after 1968 presumed, as Freud presumed, that each person is a site of constantly flowing (and thus, potentially radicalizing) sexual energy. These radicals did not think, however, that the failure of desire to find appropriate objects was at all inevitable. Instead, they focused on rescuing sexuality from its deforming sublimation into alienated labor, social normalcy, and political quietism.[24] Moreover, desire was deemed to need rescue from its parodic form in advertising discourse, where it was so hyperbolized and banal that it was thought to enervate people, to make them paradoxically stimulated, bored, and complacent.[25] This is why so much radical culture-building used Brechtian avant-garde tactics — to make strange and change the *forms* that desire was thought to take. (See, for example, Laura Mulvey's demand that the feminist avant-garde "destroy" the forms of visual pleasure, since their history is so saturated with misogyny: emancipation would only happen when the aesthetic of value animated by desire no longer valorized or

---

[24] See Alice Echols, *Daring to Be Bad: Radical Feminism in America, 1967-1975* (Minneapolis: University of Minnesota Press, 1989); Herbert Marcuse, *One-Dimensional Man* (Boston: Beacon Books, 1964) and *An Essay on Liberation* (Boston: Beacon Books, 1969); and Sohnya Sayers, Anders Stephanson, Stanley Aronowitz, and Fredric Jameson, eds., *The 60s Without Apology*, special issue of *Social Text* 9/10 (1984), esp. Stanley Aronowitz, "When the Left Was New," 11–43 and Ellen Willis, "Radical Feminism and Feminist Radicalism," 91–118.

[25] See Roland Barthes, *The Pleasure of the Text*, trans. Richard Miller (New York: Hill and Wang, 1975) and *Sade, Fourier, Loyola*, trans. Richard Miller (New York: Hill and Wang, 1976), and George Lipsitz, *Time Passages* (Minneapolis: University of Minnesota Press, 1990).

reproduced the subordination of women.) [26] This is also why the "sexual revolution" placed the emancipation of "desire" or *jouissance* (the energy of the drives that is in excess to the rational ego, fixed identities, or normative institutions) at the center of many political upheavals — against the bourgeois family, conjugal sexuality, the relation of the state to citizens, exploitation, racism, and imperialism, the place of religion and education in social life, and the place of the body in politics. The feminist dictum "The Personal is Political" sought to reiterate the centrality of desire to life: the powerful forces of desublimated, freed, or rerouted desire were frequently imagined to have the power to topple unjust conventional intimacies and entire societies. [27]

Although its history as a champion of desire might have positioned psychoanalysis as a central tool in the radical reconceptualization of society, the profession at this time came under widespread critique for serving the interests of patriarchal, capitalist, imperialist, and racist

[26] Laura Mulvey, "Visual Pleasure and Narrative Cinema," in *Visual and Other Pleasures* (1975; Bloomington: Indiana University Press, 1989), 14–29.

[27] See Hélène Cixous, "The Laugh of the Medusa," trans. Keith Cohen and Paula Cohen, in *New French Feminisms*, eds. Elaine Marks and Isabelle de Courtivon (1975; New York: Schocken Books, 1981), 245–64.

state and social institutions, including the repressive and normalizing family that shapes the world of psychoanalytic epistemology. How could a science of the individual subject have such far-reaching adverse effects? The critiques take a variety of forms. First, psychoanalysis was charged with masking its normative distinctions — between men and women and between normal and abnormal sexuality — as natural ones. These naturalized "scientific" classifications were then deployed in arguments against the legitimacy of the sexually (appetitively) disordered — heterosexual women, gays, lesbians, the urban poor, and people of color. In addition, the hierarchies implied in these classifications were put to use in imperialist arguments. [28] The elevation of imperial "civilization" over the "barbarism" of the colonized was also thought to have had

---

[28] See Partha Chatterjee, *The Nation and Its Fragments: Colonial and Postcolonial Histories* (New York: Oxford University Press, 1994); Caren Kaplan, *Questions of Travel: Postmodern Discourses of Displacement* (Durham: Duke University Press, 1996); Ann McClintock, *Imperial Leather: Race, Gender, and Sexuality in the Colonial Contest* (New York: Routledge, 1995); Doris Sommer, *Foundational Fictions: The National Romances of Latin America* (Berkeley: University of California Press, 1984); and Gayatri Chakravorty Spivak, "Acting Bits/Identity Talk," *Critical Inquiry* 18 (1992): 770–803.

implications for political supremacy within national boundaries. The symbolic and material subordination of the aforementioned so-called degenerate groups — people of color, Jews, the impoverished, and women — seemed to require theories of psychological degeneracy, deficiency, or debility, and sexuality was a prime resource for those seeking "scientific" evidence.[29]

Another side of this critique was also important to 1960s activists: psychoanalysis was available for destructive appropriation because some versions of it relied on a confusion between a notion of the universal or abstract subject and the concept of the normal or "healthy" sexual subject. Freudian "ego psychology," a U.S. variant said to encourage the unhappy subject's adaptation to normalcy, was the main target here: Wilhelm Reich, R.D. Laing, and other radical analysts of subjectivity were thought by some to offer more liberating, progressive, and non-normative notions of "mental health."[30] The hierarchies of value shielded by universalizing thought were a major

---

[29] See Sander Gilman, *Difference and Pathology: Stereotypes of Sexuality, Race, and Madness* (Ithaca: Cornell University Press, 1985) and Donna Haraway, *Simians, Cyborgs, and Women* (New York: Routledge, 1991).

[30] See Juliet Mitchell, *Psychoanalysis and Feminism* (New York: Random House, 1974).

target of radical philosophers and thinkers of the moment: the psychoanalytic profession was accordingly condemned for seeking to produce generic, universal, or "bourgeois" subjects, individuals who read the world only from the perspective of their own individuality; who learned to understand their lives solely in terms of family dynamics; who were not enabled to see themselves as subjects marked by the impersonal as well as the personal contexts of history, intimacy, power, and desire. Universal notions of "man" central to modern philosophy and other disciplines were held to have had materially damaging effects on subjectivity generally, especially for those who were considered unrepresentable in the idiom of the normal/universal. [31] In producing "scientific" knowledge that legitimated these norms of imperial personhood and species hierarchy, psychoanalysis was deemed no different than many of the human sciences and academic disciplines.

At the same time, other more ambivalent responses to the radical critique of psychoanalysis developed. Many critics, especially from the academic humanities, argued that

---

[31] See Luce Irigaray, *Speculum of the Other Woman*, trans. Gillian Gill (Ithaca: Cornell University Press, 1985) and Monique Wittig, *The Straight Mind and Other Essays* (Boston: Beacon Press, 1992).

psychoanalysis as an institution (and even Freud as a reader of his own work) actually misrepresented its own conclusions, as it produced two contradictory models of desire. One could be described by the aforementioned categories of oppressively traditional sexual difference and family role, Oedipal relations, and penis envy. The radical potential, in contrast, emanates from the model of the constantly bending, folding, and twisting incoherence of libidinal activity, all of which suggests: 1) a model of the desiring subject who is decentered or unstable; that "identity" itself, whether sexual or gendered, is therefore an always failed project in that it is always aspirational and determined by multiple, diverse and divergent aims;[32] and 2) that the libidinal energies now routed into producing narrowed versions of normal/universal and individuated identity might be rerouted toward more expansive and generous sociabilities and worlds.

---

[32] See Brennan, *The Interpretation of the Flesh* and *History after Lacan* (London: Routledge, 1993); Judith Butler, *Gender Trouble: Feminism and the Subversion of Identity* (New York: Routledge, 1990) and *Bodies That Matter* (New York: Routledge, 1993); De Lauretis, *The Practice of Love*; and Jacqueline Rose, *Sexuality in the Field of Vision* (London: Verso, 1986).

In the next few pages we will follow up on the latter prospect: that the anxieties and instabilities of desire might be made to have socially transformative consequences, for good and ill. Many of the psychoanalytically-informed theorists of desire who have pursued this line of thought rethink the ways suppressed and conventionally misrecognized desires destructively distort self- and social relations. "Identity" is, in this latter view, a mirage — a mirage of the ego that gives you an "I" and a name to protect you from being overwhelmed by the stimuli you encounter, and/or a mirage of the social order, which teaches you to renounce your desire's excess and ambivalence so that you can be intelligible under the discipline of the norms that make hierarchies of social value seem natural by rooting them in the pseudo-natural structure of hetero-sexualized sexual difference.

This version of the mirage of stable identity has been most fully thought through by Jacques Lacan and social theorists who think with his work. Lacan defines "the subject" as an effect of the anxiety that is generated by the assumption of an identity within what he calls the Symbolic Order. From this point of view the production of subjects with identities that particularize them is identical to the process of their shaping by ideology: this does not mean that there is no such thing as the enigma of personality but that persons find their form, their "selves," from within fantasy, which includes the projection of impossible desires onto love objects for a bearable and prior stability and the mediation of norms that make them socially intelligible. Identity is like a turtle shell out of which the subject keeps craning her/his neck to see if and where it might be possible to move: a way of locating, protecting, masking, and disciplining the person.

To make this argument Lacan reinterprets the split in the scene of primary desire we have already traced in Freud's work. Once the infant is forced to know her differentiation from the world, she experiences traumatic fragmentation, the instability of everything, abandonment, and loss of mastery; at the same time the infant misremembers her prior life as an experience of bodily wholeness or integrity. He suggests that she misremembers because, not only was the prior condition disorganized, appetitive, and libidinally unzoned, but also the "memory" of the prior state, which was really just an affective sense and not anything we typically understand as memory, was not even possible before the event of the break. Thus her "memory" of her lost form is retroactively constituted the way all desire and memory are, via deferral, lag, displacement, and detour, what Freud calls *Nachträglichkeit*. Lacan calls the state of misremembered self-continuity and wholeness the Imaginary, and defines the Symbolic as the condition of traumatized fragmentation in which the subject — under threat of absolute loss/castration — must attempt to but never comfortably assume language and identity to manage her environment and speak her desire (for the mother, and then for the subsequent replacements).

The Lacanian Real, which represents the unbearable and unsymbolizable limit that is sensed but always missed, puts pressure on the subject to disavow the anxiety of non-meaning that nonetheless haunts her searching for foundations or anchors in objects. The Real, one might say, exerts pressure on the drives to find objects to love, but those objects, bound to the Symbolic, are always insufficient to the pressure of fantasy that keeps one driven toward them. But if the Real is sensed, the Imaginary and the Symbolic seem bound to time, presence, and memory. The subject is said to experience these states as though they happened in chronological order — first, the Imaginary, vaguely recalled as the time of complete security before the traumatic break, desire, and language set in; then the Symbolic, the post-traumatic time of individual anxiety, desire, and speech, as well as the space of culture, ideology, hierarchy, and the abstraction of patriarchal Law. Lacan argues, however, that as the Imaginary and the Symbolic are simultaneous in the space of the subject's unconscious, but not identical to each other, their lack of fit produces the fluctuating and contradictory feelings of abjection, grandiosity, and ambivalence that the subject is fated to reconcile as "her" desire for the rest of her life.[33]

Lacan describes the Symbolic as built around the abstract and all-powerful Name of the Father (think the Wizard of Oz, before he is revealed to be just an ordinary wizard). This paternal metaphor has a number of functions: in contrast to the perfect father the child thinks she actually has, the Name of the Father is that abstract authority that defines the Laws of cultural hierarchy through language, represses the forces that destabilize order, links social and individual privilege through masculinity, and organizes value fundamentally around sexual difference. Lacan's major work begins in the post-World War II era, and the Name of the Father can be read as a description of monumentalizing fascist technologies of desire, but Lacan's base of pedagogical influence was radically expanded in the era of the '68 "revolution" when a new generation of radicals adopted his ways of describing language, desire, and violence, despite the fact that this generation was countering a different moment in the practices of transnational capitalism. Here the definition of desire as a property of

---

[33] See Victor Burgin, *In/different Spaces: Places and Memory in Visual Culture* (Berkeley: University of California Press, 1996), 179–275.

language is sutured to a view of desire as feeling organized fundamentally through and experienced as a property of sexual difference and sexuality.

In contrast to Freud's literal description of castration anxiety at the center of sexual difference and heterosexual desire, Lacan focuses on the drama of symbolic castration in the production of identity and the desire that flows in excess of it. I have described The "Name of the Father" as the place of Law in the Symbolic order of culture. It is signified by the phallus that conjoins the separation of the sexes to the authority of abstract truth. Lacan takes up the symbolic and anatomical scenarios of castration through a distinction between the phallus and the penis, in which the symbolic term (phallus) signifies all of the relations of possession one can have to the object of desire: the penis (having it or not having it; being [bearing or symbolizing] it, or not). But how abstract is the phallus? Many have argued that the phallus as the figure of the Law relies on the anatomical penis to give it form and prop it up.[34] Yet in this version of sexual difference, it is not just women whose lack subordinates them to masculinist social regimes. Men are also

---

[34] See Jane Gallop, *The Daughter's Seduction: Feminism and Psychoanalysis* (Ithaca: Cornell University Press, 1982).

subordinated to phallic masculinity. At the same time that there seems to be conventional referential continuity between the symbolic and the fleshly sign, masculinity is constantly threatened by the fragility of their linkage. In Oedipal terms, this ordeal is ceaseless, for the male child can never have the "mother" he has lost. He must possess substitute love objects and use the Law/language to master the anxiety created by his ambivalence, as that anxiety itself is the measure of his inadequacy at being well-gendered. For Lacan, therefore, sexual difference is organized not around the penis and vagina, but the *gendering of anxiety*. Neither the male nor the female ever "possesses" the phallus: it can only represent loss and desire. In Lacanian terms, however, only the woman represents the *objet a*, the unattainable Other who always exceeds the phallic value she is supposed to represent. Men live wholly in the Symbolic, insofar as they live the privilege and burden of identifying with/as the Law.

This suggests a painful contradiction within masculinity, for the very logic that authorizes the penis to be misrecognized as the Phallus or Law sentences men to experience anxieties of adequacy and dramas of failure. The price of privilege is the instability at its foundation. How, then, does psychoanalysis help us to see the contingency that is disavowed in the domains of masculine privilege? Lacan argues that if the "unconscious is that chapter of my history that is marked by a blank [or] occupied by a falsehood," the censored material is written down in monuments like the symptoms that represent on the body, in archives of memory and seemingly impersonal traces that take on uncanny values, like childhood memories, in the presumptions of language and tradition, and in narrative norms.[35] Masculinity in particular involves creating the kind of mirage of identity an impostor or impersonator enacts. The solidity of the successful performance secures the aura of masculinity as a fixed and monumental presence.[36] Yet we also know that ambivalence, anxiety, and other forms of sexual surplus are never fully absorbed into the managerial economy of gender identity: in the symbolics of conventional masculinity, uncertainty and agitation are frequently projected onto women or "Woman," who becomes figured negatively as the origin of a *threat* to masculinity and positively as *temptation* and, more fetishistically, as *resolution* to ambivalence.

In contrast, Lacan argues that, in a woman's relation to the fetish object, what she becomes in ordinary masculine desire is a relation of

[35] Jacques Lacan, *Ecrits*, trans. Alan Sheridan (New York: W.W. Norton, 1977), 46–50.

[36] Joan Copjec, *Read My Desire: Lacan Against the Historicists* (Cambridge: MIT Press, 1994), 234.

masquerade: she must wear the mask to be intelligibly feminine, but because she is not fully absorbed by the Symbolic, she can reveal more or less of the artificiality of her mask. This is a direct contrast to the impostor the male-identified man must be in order to obscure the difference between his penis and the Phallus: because the impostor must seem natural in the identity he expresses, there can be little "play" in the expression of masculinity. But, Lacan argues, if women are subordinated by the threat they represent to the authority of the Phallus/penis they are also the excess, the irreducible difference, that cannot be managed by its regime. This exorbitant material, which is associated with "Woman" and exceeds the order of the Symbolic, is also called *jouissance* and abjection: that sublime affect which shatters or overwhelms the subject's stability in language, identity and therefore also in society.[37] In this conceptualization, women are positioned to generate a radically different kind of language, law, and desire.[38]

---

[37] See Hélène Cixous, "The Laugh of the Medusa," trans. Keith Cohen and Paula Cohen, *Signs* 1.4 (1976): 875–93; Julia Kristeva, *Powers of Horror: Essays in Abjection*, trans. Leon S. Roudiez (1980; New York: Columbia University Press, 1982); and Lacan, *Feminine Sexuality*, eds. Rose and Mitchell.

[38] Lacan, *Feminine Sexuality*, eds. Rose and Mitchell, 162–71.

There has been a vast literature of feminist response to Lacan from within psychoanalysis, arguing that the abstraction "the Name of the Father" is really just the ideology of male supremacy in newly-inscribed monumental form, or arguing that if a patriarchal identity form requires "Woman" to mirror it, then "Woman" is, after all, the holder of the Law. [39] In addition, the heterosexual presumptiveness of his model of desire has generated incisive critique.[40] Yet Lacan's theoretical sundering of the Phallus from the penis has also productively informed feminist and LGBTQ work: since the cultural rules of intelligibility and value that over-organize desire into relations of identity are not considered invariably attached to particular bodies (e.g., the Phallus does not equal the penis), as in Freud; and since masquerade and imposture seem to describe the relations of people to gender identity, it has been suggested that gender and sexuality are really the *effects* of identification or citation.[41] It

---

[39] See Rose, "Introduction II," in *Feminine Sexuality*, eds. Rose and Mitchell, 27–57, and Slavoj Žižek, *The Metastases of Enjoyment: Six Essays on Woman and Causality* (London: Verso, 1994).

[40] See Judith Roof, *A Lure of Knowledge: Lesbian Sexuality and Theory* (New York: Columbia University Press, 1991).

[41] See Judith Butler, *Gender Trouble: Feminism and the Subversion of Identity* (New York: Routledge,

has also been used to explain why live sexualities and sexually racialized non-normative
embodiments represent such a threat to powerful interests. Males adopt masculinity by citing
the normative practices they see men do; the
same goes for females; the same goes for
heterosexuals who mobilize conventional gender classifications.[42] But, inevitably, the sexual
subject will always fail to be the generic one.[43]
In this sense the linkage between conventional
gendering and failure feels both melodramatic
and mundane: what are the consequences if you
try to "quote" the normal practices identified
with your gender and you fail (think about
Superman, *The House of Mirth*, *The Bluest Eye*,
Vertigo, *Boys Don't Cry*)? What if you succeed in
gendering yourself all too well, taking on your

1990) and *Bodies That Matter: On the Discursive
Limits of "Sex"* (New York: Routledge, 1993); Lee
Edelman, *Homographesis: Essays in Gay Literary and
Cultural Theory* (New York: Routledge, 1993); Leo
Bersani and Adam Phillips, *Intimacies* (Chicago:
University of Chicago Press, 2008); and Antonio
Viego, *Dead Subjects: Toward a Politics of Loss in
Latino Studies* (Durham: Duke University Press,
2007).

[42] For non-heteronormative patriarchal kinship, see
Gilbert H. Herdt, *Same Sex, Different Cultures: Gays
and Lesbians Across Cultures* (Boulder: Westview
Press, 1997).

[43] See Rose, *Sexuality in the Field of Vision*.

gendered identity as a fetish, a monumental substitute that tries to repress your anxiety about vulnerability, loss, and failure (think *Dracula*, *Madame Bovary*, *Blade Runner*)? The dramatic scenario of aspirational gender performance that I just outlined is ordinary life for many. Is not this scenario of gender and desire also the modern story of adolescent romance (as Thompson writes about in *Going All the Way*)?

Judith Butler's anti-normative view of sexuality, which follows from these kinds of questions, contends that if the laws of sexual and gender identity are collectively "misquoted" or re-distorted by the abjected or marginalized subjects who refuse subordination to them, then the representational rules of those laws and norms can change.[44] Indeed the centrality of failure, negativity, and partial successes in the striving for gender to provide the foundation it promises but always fails to be is the condition for its symbolic and practical transformation. But a historical view of this optimistic scenario reminds us how much performative variation a dominant regime can absorb into its normative domain: for these citational changes on gender to reverberate as

---

[44] Butler, *Bodies That Matter*; see also Mary Ann Doane, *Femmes Fatales: Feminism, Film Theory, Psychoanalysis* (New York: Routledge, 1991).

social critique of the law and for other subjects, a political context that amplifies them and links them to other transformative practices needs to exist. In addition, as suggested earlier, all men do not live the privilege of the patriarchalized "Phallus" identically; nor does the fiction of "Woman" in the Symbolic limit or mark all women in the same way: racism, colonialism, heteronormativity, class entitlement, and other forms of hierarchy interfere with the fantasy that sexual difference has a universal meaning.[45] Despite their critical relation to the psychoanalytic tradition, thinkers in the Lacanian genealogy tend to work within its tendency to flatten out the difference in scale, intensity, and value that different kinds of events have on the subject. In any case, we see here an important transformation in the history of the idea of subjectivity: the model of

---

[45] See Elizabeth Abel, Barbara Christian, and Helene Moglen, eds,. *Female Subjects in Black and White: Race, Psychoanalysis, Feminism* (Berkeley: University of California Press, 1997); Lillian Faderman, *Odd Girls and Twilight Lovers: A History of Lesbian Life in Twentieth Century America* (New York: Columbia University Press, 1991); Hortense J. Spillers, "Mama's Baby, Papa's Maybe: An American Grammar Book," *Diacritics* 17 (1987): 64–81; Spivak, "Acting Bits/Identity Talks"; and Carolyn Kay Steedman, *Landscape for a Good Woman: A Story of Two Lives* (Newark: Rutgers University Press, 1986).

soulful universal rationality that defines the paradigmatic Enlightenment subject is supplanted by a model of the human who is not only destabilized by conflicting and powerful drives, but by the contradictory exigencies of identity as such. Sexual politics wagers that these contradictions can be made productive rather than paralyzing and repetitious — given the right material conditions for transformative consciousness and practice.

Another vital tradition of anti-psychoanalytic thought criticizes psychoanalysis in the name of desire's irregularity, excess, and incoherence, but this time the critique focuses on moving beyond notions of the bodily ego or identity entirely. Focusing on the *surface* or *topographical* trajectories of the *body*, Gilles Deleuze and Félix Guattari, Elizabeth Grosz, and others talk about the way the attachments that desire engenders constantly reorganize the body into a state(s) of "becoming," which in turn radically reshape the body as an erotic zone, a zone of meaning, value, and power.[46]

---

[46] See Gilles Deleuze and Félix Guattari, *Anti-Oedipus: Capitalism and Schizophrenia,* trans. Robert Hurley, Mark Seem, and Helen Lane (New York: Viking Press, 1977); Elizabeth A. Grosz, *Volatile Bodies: Toward a Corporeal Feminism* (Bloomington: Indiana University Press, 1994); Camilla Griggers, *Becoming-Woman* (Minneapolis: University of Minn-

They use the language of "deterritorialization" and "reterritorialization" to describe the process by which desire undoes the zone of its identity and then remakes itself according to the mode in which it lands in a new space and "civilizes" it. In this view desire attaches itself to forms that, in turn, have an impact on the desiring subject, reorganizing its self-relation, changing the form and the spaces of its desire. The more attachments, the more transformation: the "rhizomatics" of desire produce a model of embodied affect constantly branching out. Genital sexuality in this view no longer has to organize the bodily senses, and both personal and political histories are therefore opened to practices beyond the violence of the "molar" (supposedly unified and bounded) identity form and institutional desire.

Capitalist notions of product and profit, which have intensified their organization and exploitation of the body during the last century, would also be overturned by this notion of the subject who becomes an entity outside of the triangulated Oedipal "Mommy-Daddy-Me" prison of psychoanalysis. This radical way of reading the subject's construction by her desire not only refuses the view that the subject is a traumatized infantile core knotted up by the

---

esota Press, 1997); and Elspeth Probyn, *Outside Belongings* (New York: Routledge, 1996).

compulsion to repeat a normative erotic organization, but also produces ways of reading sensation that has the subject's affect inevitably exceeding the normal and proper codes that try to organize her, as she moves through the world becoming impacted by and different within the event of her encounters. On the other hand, as we have seen, desire's restless drive toward finding spaces and shapes will always be met if not overmatched by the coercive and seductive forms of propriety, virtue, and discipline that organize societies, and individual will cannot dissolve these by force or by theory. What is the status of desire's excesses for the individual or social order, then? Can anything general be said about it?

Questions like this have brought under fire the concept of "desire" itself as a useful political or analytic tool. Critics like Michel Foucault and Gayle Rubin remove individual desire from the center of the analysis of sexuality. Instead, they focus on the practices of *populations* that are made socially visible in institutionally complex fields of power, like cities, prisons, clinics, and nations. In this view, "sexuality" is not what it often seems to be, the sum of the erotic desires and practices with which a person identifies, and which a person can express as if from the core of her being; nor is it the process of libidinization we have been tracking in the Freudian or Lacanian context. Sexuality does not emerge naturally from subjects, in Foucault's view. It is a field of normative bodily and affective practices with which subjects are taught to identify and about which they are taught to speak — to the church, the state, the medical profession, and especially to psycho-analysts. It is produced by institutional and ideological relations between experience, know-ledge, and power. A culture of individuating but institutionally-inflected confession has grown up to engender "sexuality" which, Foucault says, is a form of discourse about "desire" and the genital practices that are said to express it: he argues that the main organs of modern sexuality are the mouth and the ear. From this perspective, the drives, desire, and pleasures are under-described by the normative discourse called "sexuality."

But this does not mean that sexuality is merely an effect of implanted institutional domination. It is a historicizable and relational concept that can be traced to the emergence of modern classificatory institutions. Until rela-tively recently, sexual identity was not even an idea about desire's form, or a way of taxono-mizing and disciplining people. For example, there may always have been people with same-sex desire and people who performed same-sex sex acts, but historians of sexuality tell us that the categories "homosexuality" and "heterosexuality" were invented in the 1890's as a part of a general movement to classify perverts or the non-normal in order to construct the terms of the modern, civilized individuality to which we have already referred. In other words, the unity of sexual desire, sexual identity, and sexual practice that "moderns" take as given in the late twentieth century has never been a "fact" of personhood at all.[47]

---

[47] See Chauncey, *Gay New York*; Janet Halley, "The Politics of the Closet: Legal Articulation of Sexual Orientation Identity," in *After Identity: A Reader in Law and Culture*, ed. Dan Daniels and Karen Engle (New York: Routledge, 1995), 24–38; David Halperin, *How to Do the History of Homosexuality* (Chicago: University of Chicago Press, 2002); and Jonathan Ned Katz, *The Invention of Heterosexuality* (New York: Dutton, 1995). See also Glenn Burger's *Chaucer's Queer Nation* (Minneapolis: University of Minnesota Press, 2003); L.O. Aranye Fradenburg, *Sacrifice Your Love: Psychoanalysis, Historicism, Chaucer* (Minneapolis: University of Minnesota Press, 2002); Louise Fradenburg and Carla Freccero, eds., *Premodern Sexualities* (New York: Routledge, 1996); Jonathan Goldberg and Madhavi Menon, "Queering History," *PMLA* 120.5 (2005): 1608–617; Karma Lochrie, *Heterosyncracies: Female Sexuality When Normal Wasn't* (Minneapolis: University of Minnesota Press, 2005); and Karma Lochrie, Peggy McCracken, and James Schultz, *Constructing Medieval Sexuality* (Minneapolis: University of Minnesota Press, 1997).

LOVE

The entry on "Desire" mainly focused on the organization of the drives into object-anchored desires, orientations, and styles of relating. Explanations of desire were organized by various psychoanalytic accounts of attachment, identity and affect, and this book tells briefly the recent history of their importance in critical theory and practice. This entry, on Love, begins with an excursion into fantasy, moving away from the familial scene of psychoanalysis and examining the encounter of unconscious fantasy with the theatrical or scenic structure of normative fantasy. Whether viewed psycho-analytically, institutionally, or ideologically, in this entry love is deemed always an outcome of fantasy. Without fantasy, there would be no love. There would be no way to move through the uneven field of our ambivalent attachments to our sustaining objects, which possess us and thereby dispossess us of our capacity to idealize ourselves or them as consistent and benign simplicities. Without repairing the cleavages, fantasy makes it possible not to be destroyed by all that.

We will pursue different notions of love by way of some of the workings of romance in personal life and commodity culture, the places where subjects learn to populate fantasy with foundational material for building worlds and lives.

§ FANTASY

Foucault's vision of a non-institutionalized mode of pleasure untethered to symbolization or norms brings us to a final form desire is said to take in psychoanalytic theory. This is the concept of *fantasy*. What Freudians and Lacanians mean by fantasy is not what one might expect. In popular culture, fantasy is a dreamy narrative that brackets realism and without entirely departing from it, connects up a desiring subject with her ideal or nightmare object, whereas in Freudian psychoanalysis fantasy takes the shape of unconscious wishes that invest images with the force of their ordering impulse and, in certain instances, convert them into symptoms; Laplanche and Pontalis then move through Lacan to call fantasy the *setting* for desire's enactment, a setting in which desire gets caught up in sequences of image and action that are not the same thing as their manifest representation.[48]

This means that to comprehend fantasy we need to move between unconscious structurations of desire and the conventions meant to sanitize them into an intention. After all, the fundamental gift-message of modern popular culture, "You are not alone," pretends that this fact is a simple relief. Yet we know that this gift is overwhelming. It at once valorizes the subject's uniqueness and her general qualities: it asserts that she is deserving of a kind of pleasure that feels both like recognition and a victory over something; and that she is sovereign and dependent on her objects to achieve that aim, among other things. The whole cluster of tendencies is fulfilled in all sorts of action films, whether the tenor of survival is at a large or small scale. If we think of romance as a genre of action film, in which an intensity of the need to survive is played out by a series of dramatic pursuits, actions, and pacifications, then the romance plot's setting for fantasy can be seen as less merely

---

[48] See de Lauretis, *The Practice of Love*; Cora Kaplan, "*The Thorn Birds*: Fiction, Fantasy, Femininity," in *Formations of Fantasy*, eds. Victor Burgin, James Donald, and Cora Kaplan (London: Methuen, 1986), 142–66; and Laplanche and Pontalis, *The Language of Psychoanalysis*.

conventional and more about the plotting of
intensities that hold up a world that the
unconscious deems worth living in.

Take, for example, the work marketed as
"the greatest love story of all time," *Gone With
the Wind*. Readers of this novel and viewers of
this film typically see the relation of Scarlett
O'Hara and Rhett Butler as the perfection of
romantic fantasy because each meets a passionate match in the other, and because even
though their great love fails, it *is* a great love
that stands the test of time and marks the
lovers permanently.[49] It does not matter that
the man understands the woman entirely, while
the woman has no clue about herself, or him:
indeed, Rhett is a better man *and* woman than
Scarlett. *Gone with the Wind* may stretch gender
norms in the characters' pursuit of economic
and romantic aims, but the novel maintains
throughout the romantic rule that gives license
to the man, who wears it as physical and
psychological superiority. But a scene- and
sense-oriented reading of the fantasy at play in
this work might suggest that desire is played
out in a *compulsion to repeat* variations on a
fantasy tableau: a tableau of mutual love at
first sight that always leads to a circuit of

---

[49] See Helen Taylor, *Scarlett's Women: Gone with the
Wind and its Female Fans* (New Brunswick: Rutgers
University Press, 1989).

passionate battle, seduction, disappointment, and desire (in this case, because whenever one lover feels love the other feels hard or defensive). The elaboration of this core in a spectacular epic tale of romance, devastation, and survival set against the backdrop of the American Civil War, and especially Sherman's scorched-earth march through the South, then mirrors the personal plot in the political one. All of this suggests that, in *Gone with the Wind*, heterosexual romance and sovereign nationality require fantasy to work its magic on subjects, generating an optimism that both plays out ambivalence and disavows complexity. *Gone with the Wind* narrates the compulsion to repeat as a relation between a sensual utopia (here, the Confederacy, romantic intimacy) and a jumble of obstacles that must be narratively mastered so that the utopia might be approached once again. *The scene of desire and the obstacles to it become eroticized, rather than the love that seems to motor it.* "Tomorrow is another day," the text's famous platitude, converts the fantasy scene of love for persons and worlds into a scene of the love of cliché, of repetition itself.

This kind of interpretive shift from couple-oriented desire to the erotics of a scene of encounter with the fantasy requires repositioning the desiring subject as a *spectator* as well as a participant in her scene of desire, and suggests a kind of doubleness the subject must have in her relation to pursuing her pleasure.

John Berger has suggested one version of this relation of doubleness: because women are the primary objects of sexualization in heterosexual culture, they learn to identify both as desiring subjects and as objects of desire. Berger illustrates this split with the tableau of a woman who walks across a room and imagines, as she does so, being watched navigating the space.[50]But the psychoanalytic claim about the subject as spectator to her desire is even more mobile and divided than Berger would allow. The centrality of repetition to pleasure and of deferral to desire indeed places the desiring subject *in* her story, and well as makes her a reader *of* her story. These two forms, acting and interpretation, enable the desiring subject to reinhabit her own plot from a *number* of imaginary vantage points, simultaneously.

Laplanche and Pontalis's "Fantasy and the Origins of Sexuality" has been especially influential in establishing this view of the specificity of fantasy-work in the production of desire.[51] They argue that fantasies are scenes into which the subject unconsciously translates herself in order to experience, in multiple ways, the desire released by the originary sexual

---

[50] John Berger, *Ways of Seeing* (London: Penguin Books, 1972).

[51] Jean Laplanche and Jean-Bertrand Pontalis, "Fantasy and the Origins of Sexuality," in *Formations of Fantasy*, eds. Burgin, Donald, and Kaplan, 5–34.

trauma and the paradoxical, ambivalent attachments it generates. Fantasy donates a sense of affective coherence to what is incoherent and contradictory in the subject; provides a sense of reliable continuity amidst the flux of intensities and attachments; and allows out-of-sync-ness and unevenness of being in the ordinary world at once to generate a secure psychotic enclave and to maintain the subject's openness to the ordinary disturbances of experience.

To think this way about the manifestations of fantasy is to change how we have been defining the sexual and desiring subject. We are no longer solely negotiating a passage of desire between the infant and her mother, or the adult and the sexual objects that later come to substitute for the traumatically lost mother. We are focusing now on the space of desire, in a field of scenes, tableaux, episodes, and events. Fantasy is the place where the subject encounters herself already negotiating the social. The origin of fantasy may still be the trauma of infantile separation — that's one theory. However we account for its origins, though, it's clear that the subjectivity desire makes is fundamentally incited by *external* stimuli that make a dent on the subject. The affective disturbance can reassemble one's usual form in any number of shapes or elaborations: in personal styles of seduction, anxious or confident attachment, confusion, shame, dread, optimism, self- or other-directed pleasure, for example. Or in stories about who one is and what one wants, stories to which one clings so as to be able to re-encounter oneself as solid and in proximity to being idealizable.

It is often said therefore that the desiring subject is well served by the formalism of desire: although desire is anarchic and restless, the objects to which desire becomes attached stabilize the subject and enable her to assume a stable-enough identity. In this model a person is someone who is retroactively created: you know who you "are" only by interpreting where your desire has already taken you. But we have already seen that your desire does not take you to its predestined object, the thing that will repair the trauma (of maternal separation, of sexual difference) that set you on your voyage in the first place. Desire is practical: it takes what it can get. Desire has bad eyesight, as it were: remember, that the object is not a thing, but a cluster of fantasmic investments in a scene that represents itself as offering some traction, not a solution to the irreparable con-tradictions of desire. On your behalf, in an effort to release you from abandonment to autoeroticism — or, more precisely, to restore your autoeroticism to sociability — your desire *misrecognizes* a given object as that which will restore you to something that you sense effectively as a hole in you. Your object, then, does not express transparently who you "are" but says *something* about what it takes for you to anchor yourself in space and time. Meanwhile the story of your life becomes the story of the detours your desire takes.[52]

Freud's "A Child is Being Beaten," the master text for this line of thought, proposes that when the subject fantasizes scenes of desire she takes multiple positions in those scenes: in this case, a patient says she hears a young boy being beaten in the next room, and she identifies as the beater, the beaten, the spectator, the eavesdropper. Each of the positions in the scene of fantasy connects to a different aspect of the desiring subject's senses and sense of power; the grandiosity of the fantasy enables the subject to saturate mentally all experience and all feeling. Earlier I described the ways in which romance narrative turns erotic ambivalence into serial experience by spacing out desire, obstacle, and romantic overcoming in the intervals of narrative time. The post-Freudian model of fantasy as the scene of desire provides another way of representing ambivalence without its internal tensions: rather than tracking conflicting aims among the various kinds of attachment the subject feels, the scenic form of fantasy enables the desiring subject to produce a series of interpretations that do not have to cohere as a narrative, but that nonetheless make up the scene. This model of

---

[52] See Sedgwick, "A Poem Is Being Written."

the subject demands reading the way a photograph, or a hieroglyph does: it requires multiple strands of causal narration. This is what Freud meant by *overdetermination*: to be overdetermined is to see oneself and one's objects of interest as the point of convergence of many forces. This model of a thing's multiple causation explains how, despite our wild affects and thoughts, we retain a fantasmatic sense of reliability and solidity; it explains how we can maintain conflicting ideas of who we and our objects are without collapsing or going psychotic.

Take, for example, the scene of intimate ambivalence par excellence: infidelity. In the real life of normative intimacy the different relationships brought into competitive proximity in infidelity are frequently revealed via tableaux or scenic-ness. Someone walks into a room at the wrong time; or someone cannot get out of her mind the image of the adulterous sex; someone cannot forget the way the room looked when she came into the unhappy knowledge. The cheating lover may be occupying multiple positions in the scene: the lover, the beloved, the guilty one, the injurer, the agent, the victim. If the adulterer opines that she is cheating because her primary relationship has failed her miserably, she is using the logic of romance narrative to split apart the scene of ambivalence: distressed couple, happy infidelity. But if the caught or confessing wanderer insists to her partner and her lover that neither relationship has anything to do with the other, she is arguing from the logic of fantasy, protecting all positions as sites of her own desire. Her explanation cannot be called *false* if the sexual wanderer experiences the scene this way: neither is it true in the sense that the interpretation adequately explains the tangle of motives and impulses that produced her acts. This is why fantasy and romantic narrative generally are best described as structures of *psychical reality*, neither true nor false where facts are concerned, but affectively true insofar as the compulsion to repeat that organizes it is the reality through which the subject projects desire and processes experience.[53]

As with all animating forms, this model of fantasy implies a theory of the subject. But it repudiates completely the model of the subject whose desire is the truth of her identity and whose actions are the expressions of her desire. The subject (of fantasy) might be read instead as the place where the fragmentation of the subject produced by primal trauma is expressed through repetition: this is the Freudian view, and it directs our attention to the drama of

---

[53] See Laplanche and Pontalis, *The Language of Psychoanalysis*, and Kaplan, "*The Thorn Birds*: Fiction, Fantasy, Femininity."

small differences through which the subject attempts to master her "normal" and her "perverse" inclinations. But the scene of fantasy can also be said to reveal the fundamental non-coherence of the subject, to which violence is done by the demands of the identity form, and which may well play out a competition between the subject's desire to be recognized by her object and her desire to destroy the object she desires.[54] Either of these models (mastery, destructive/reparative impulses) can be seen in the ways that the subject takes up patterning with respect to her objects. In any case, because people are distinguished to themselves, their intimates, and in history by their particular structures and styles of repetition, the subject becomes coherent and inhabits her identity only as she repeats an attachment to a scene that features her self-performance. But how do we understand this in more political or social terms? Foucault argues that ideologies of the *normal* turn certain subjects into a "population" by way of the taxonomic state, the corporealized hierarchies of capitalism, and medical, legal, educational, and religious practices. Subjects who become intelligible within these regimes of normativity are trained to repeat identification with particular fantasy forms, which is to say that they

---

[54] See Klein and Rivière, *Love, Hate, and Reparation*.

are incited to identify with some repetitions and styles over other ones. In this sense the promise of social belonging casts Enlightenment ideologies of happiness, individual autonomy and uniqueness, and freedom in terms of normative conventionality. As a result, some critics argue that even normalized or conventional social relationships can be perverse, in that their fulfillment can entail implicit or underdeveloped fantasies of bucking social convention: in this Marxist/psychoanalytic tradition of thought, conventions themselves are placeholders for desired political as well as personal transformation beyond the horizon of the ordinary appearances and immediate sensations of belonging.[55]

---

[55] See Lauren Berlant, "'68, or Something," *Critical Inquiry* 21 (1994): 124–55 and *The Queen of America Goes to Washington City: Essays on Sex and Citizenship* (Durham: Duke University Press, 1997); Fredric Jameson, "Reification and Utopia in Mass Culture," *Social Text* 1 (1979): 130–48; and Oskar Negt and Alexander Kluge, *Public Sphere and Experience: Toward an Analysis of the Bourgeois and Proletarian Public Sphere* (Minneapolis: University of Minnesota Press, 1993).

§ DESIRE, NARRATIVE, COMMODITY, THERAPY

still image from *Marnie* (dir. Alfred Hithcock, 1964)

Alfred Hitchcock's *Marnie* (1964) tells the story of a woman who appears to hate men, but who uses her competence and her beauty in a way that has the structure of a seduction. Efficient in the office and icily striking, she so bewitches her bosses that, vulnerable with desire, they relax their managerial rules around her: when they manifest this double vulnerability she absconds with their money. This is the back-story of the film's first scene: we enter as the police interview a Mr. Strutt, who has been both aroused and embezzled by Marnie (played by Tippi Hedren). Here is the first thing he, or anyone, says about her: "That little witch. I'll have her put away for twenty years. I knew she was too good to be true. Always so eager to work overtime, never made a mistake, always pulling her skirt down over her knees as though they were a national treasure."

You would call Marnie a plain seductress, were it not that her confidence game always bleeds beyond the scene of the crime to other disturbed places, spaces of antithetical power and abjection. Each time she steals she changes identity, takes a brief vacation to ride her prized horse, and brings gifts and funds to her mother, who thinks that she has triumphed legitimately in the financial world.

What to make of this pattern, this woman? At the start we think Marnie might be evil: in the five opening minutes before the film shows her face, it shows her body remaking its feminine style and choosing from among several legal identities. That femininity is the scene of her disruption is figured in the way she hides fraudulent Social Security cards in the secret compartment of a gold reticule. But we soon see that Marnie has been subject to trauma, and that her repeated routine is a circuitous way of seducing, not men, but her mother — to love her, protect her, accept her, repair her blockages to manifesting maternal love. It turns out that Marnie killed a man when she was young, a drunk and menacing client of her prostitute mother's, and that her mother took the rap for it: the memory half-repressed by Marnie's traumatic amnesia and her mother's cold and protective silence about the event is figured constantly by symptoms such as panic attacks, nightmares, and sexual frigidity, which, unlike Marnie herself, never seem to lie.

still image from *Marnie* (dir. Alfred Hitchcock, 1964)

But Marnie meets up with a man who is her match. Along with running a business, Mark Rutland (played by Sean Connery) studies animal instincts (zoology, entomology, and marine biology) and specializes in engendering "trust." He falls for Marnie during the first panic attack he sees, and as he learns of the criminal ways in which she has made men "pay" for the sex they never had, he pays back the debts her robberies have incurred. Then Rutland focuses on fixing her sexual problem: he exploits her fear of prison to trap her into a marriage, and eventually rapes her in their honeymoon bedroom. Then, hastily acquiring some psychoanalytic expertise, through books like *Sexual Aberrations of the Criminal Female*, *Frigidity in Women*, and *The Psychopathic Delinquent and Criminal*, he compels Marnie to renounce her aversion to intimacy and to beg him for help: in turn, he enables her "real" story to come out in the open, and accomplishes healing through the narrative conversion of trauma to love.

Marnie's closing lines in the film, "I don't want to go to jail, Mark. I want to stay with you," confirm both parodically and sincerely the husband's sense that romance and the psychological sciences use much the same contract to aid the impaired subject, the one who desires but cannot achieve entry into a love plot: in this contract, a masterful subject tells a more vulnerable one that he will enable her to assume a full and sustaining identity if she devotes herself entirely to inhabiting the intimate scene he prepares for her. At first Marnie refuses the terms of this exchange, designating them as tools that use money and institutional power to advance the sexual entitlement of men. As Marnie remarks mockingly, "You Freud, Me Jane." But *Marnie* also suggests that to be healthy the woman must conclude that consent to the normative contract of intimacy is indeed the condition of her happiness, and that the terms of her earlier protests were a part of her mental illness. Marnie does this by coming to believe, nonsensically, that Mark's judgment and love will produce for her a clean break with the past, and thus return to her her "own" story. This fantasy of narrative repair suggests that psychoanalysis is the science of desire's shattering and traumatic history, while romance involves magical thinking about desire's future. It matters not that Hitchcock might have seen all of this resolution ironically or that he might have sadistically identified with both protagonists. What matters is that this transfer from the epistemology of symptom to that of repair through love's genre is conventional, and does not read as avant-garde or unintelligible.

Marnie's gendered distribution of thera-peutic modes suggests that the conventional narratives and institutions of romance share with psychoanalysis many social and socializing functions. As sites for theorizing and imaging desire, they manage ambivalence; designate the individual as the unit of social transformation; reduce the overwhelming world to an intensi-fied space of personal relations; establish dramas of love, sexuality, and reproduction as the dramas central to living; and install the institutions of intimacy (most explicitly the married couple and the intergenerational family) as the proper sites for providing the life plot in which a subject has "a life" and a future. That these forms are conventions whose imaginary propriety serves a variety of religious and capitalist institutions does not mean that the desire for romantic love is an ignorant or false desire: indeed, these conventions express important needs to feel unconflicted and to possess some zone where intimacy can flourish. But in the modern United States, and the places its media forms influence, to different degrees, the fantasy world of romance is used normatively — as a rule that legislates the boundary between a legitimate and valuable mode of living/loving and all the others. The reduction of life's legitimate possibility to one plot is the source of romantic love's terrorizing, coercive, shaming, manipulative, or just diminishing effects — on the imagination as well as on practice.

Most important to this essay is addressing the ways that fantasies of romantic love and of therapy posit norms of gender and sexuality as threats to people's flourishing and yet themselves are part of the problem for which they offer themselves as a solution. It's not just that psychoanalysis has tended to organize the world around the scene that gives privilege to modes of embodiment, anxiety, and authority that serve straight men's interests in maintaining (even a contingent) privilege; at the same time, popular romance, pretending no science, arranges the world around hetero-feminine experiences and desires for intimacy.

In each discourse, the sexual other is deemed, *a priori*, to be emotionally inadequate. Of course, people of any gender rarely or barely inhabit these ideals fully or unambivalently,[56] but these ideals nonetheless mark the horizons of fantasy and fulfilled identity by which people come to measure their lives or process their confusions. The institutions and ideologies of romantic/familial love declare woman/women to be the arbiters, sources, managers, agents, and victims of intimacy: the love plots that saturate the public sphere are central vehicles for reproducing normative or "generic" femininity. In this next segment of our investigation of desire/fantasy, we will focus on its romantic commodities: first, on some of its popular narrative forms and second, on three related kinds of popular culture that organize the conventional meanings of desire, gender, and sexuality: therapy culture, commodity culture, and liberal political culture.

So far in this book desire has appeared as an ambivalent energy organized by processes of attachment. It manifests an enormously

---

[56] See Sedgwick, *Epistemology of the Closet*.

optimistic drive to generate sustained intimate contact. But its typical forms are also said to be motivated by psychic trauma, associated with perversion and melancholic masochism, and structured by dramas of incest, castration, shame, and guilt. In the popular culture of romance such instability and ambivalence are always shaped by the girdle of love. These dramas are always formed in relation to a fantasy that desire, in the form of love, will make life more simple, not crazier. Boy meets girl, boy loses girl, boy gets girl: this generic sequence structures countless narratives both high and low (sometimes with the genders reversed).[57]

The fantasy forms that structure popular love discourse constantly express the desire for love to simplify living. The content of these narratives is, in a sense, just a surface variation on a narrowly-constructed theme: love's clarifying wash is expressed positively, in bright-eyed love stories, and negatively, in narratives that track failure at intimacy in the funereal tones of tragedy or the biting tones of cynical realism. Even when ambivalence organizes a narrative, keeping desire and negativity in close quarters, love is often named as the

---

[57] See the film *Boy Meets Girl* (dir. Lloyd Bacon, 1938), a tale about the representational conventions and effects of Hollywood's obsession with romance.

disappointing thing that ought to have stabilized these antithetical drives. Thus in the wish for romance, love plots insist on a law for desire. But the law is, as usual, contradictory. In the popular rhetoric of romance, love is a most fragile thing, a supposed selflessness in a world full of self; its plots also represent the compulsion to repeat scenes of transgression, ruthlessness, and control, as well as their resolution into something transcendent, or at least consoling, still, stabilized — at least for a moment.

The pseudo-clarities of sexual difference play a large part in conventionalizing this relation of risk and fantasy. Love plots are marked by a longing for love to have the power to make the loved one transparent, and therefore a safe site on which to place one's own desire without fear of its usual unsettling effects. The trope of "love at first sight" expresses this wish as well: when I saw you, it was as though I had lived my whole life in a moment — I knew, then, my fate. The contemporary bestseller *The Bridges of Madison County* expresses this set of desires, but not because they are conventional: the fictive author's frame narrative marks the story as a revolutionary repudiation of a culture that has hardened to love's transformative and self-realizing potential. Its protagonists, Robert Kincaid and Francesca Johnson, do not experience love at first sight, but feel so inexorably drawn toward each other that they soon "know" that all of human history has worked to bring them together and given them instant mutual knowledge. To express the feeling that love has finally brought them what love is supposed to bring everyone, the book uses a language of ghostliness and haunting: for the feeling of love that they had both cherished and relinquished as they grew older and disappointed now returns like a ghost, a transparent body that haunts *them*, infuses their lives with a spirit. When they make love, which they do for just a few long days before Francesca's husband returns, all of material life dissolves into "shape and sound and shadow"; their language breaks down into elemental "small, unintelligible sounds."[58] The perfect asociality of their intimacy means that when Robert leaves Francesca they can experience their love for the rest of their lives as a perfect object, an animating ghost that was true to their desire.

The wish this novella expresses — that a man would come to a woman and understand her without aggressive probing; that he would be critical of masculinity without being ashamed of it or himself; that he would be capable of both hardness and softness, and that this would provide a context for the woman to

---

[58] Robert James Waller, *The Bridges of Madison County* (New York: Warner Books, 1992), 108.

experience herself as freely as he does — is the structural stuff of popular romance. The story that love is invulnerable to the instabilities of narrative or history, and is a beautifully shaped web of lyrical mutuality, is at the ideological core of modern heterosexuality. It enables heterosexuality to be construed as a relation of desire that expresses people's true feelings. It says nothing of the institutions and ideologies that police it (in *Bridges* the local community has a sharp nose for adultery). To the degree that a love story pits lyrical feelings about intimacy against the narrative traumas engendered in ordinary or public life, it participates in the genre of romance: the love plot provides a seemingly non-ideological resolution to the fractures and contradictions of history. The mix of utopianism and amnesia this suggests is, as we have previously said, the fetish-effect of fantasy.

But what about the many times when love fails to sustain a concrete life context and the identities shaped within it? What about the times when the intimate other remains opaque to the desiring subject? Why are the transparency and simultaneity promised by love not automatically considered a mirage and a fraud, given the frequency with which this wish is disconfirmed by experience? It should not be surprising to learn that narratives of romantic failure are dedicated, frequently and paradoxically, to reanimating the belief in love's promise to structure both conventional life and the magical life of intimate mutuality across distance and difference. Toni Morrison's *Sula* frames two such moments, in each of which the fetish of a transparent, transcendent experience of desire is marked by an extreme, absorbing, death-driven melancholia.

Most famously, *Sula* has been called a lesbian novel, for the relations between Sula and her friend Nel organize everything good about their lives. (Not much is good about their lives except their friendship, really: they live during a period of severe economic distress and racial subordination in the United States between World War I and World War II.) Because there are no institutions or ideologies to give them sustaining language and contexts for their intimacy, and because heterosexuality names the structure of living for them, Sula dies before Nel realizes that Sula was her most intimate partner all along. Nel then releases an elemental howl (much like the murmuring sounds in *Bridges*) that figures the transparent truth of their mutual love, a love that can only be lived as the memory of something that did not happen, after history has reached its limit.

In contrast, Sula experiences this desire for transparency in the real time of love — but not with Nel. It is with her lover, Ajax, the man with whom, as a young adolescent, she had first experienced sexual excitement. Later in life they become lovers. To Sula this means wanting to know everything about him, which is the same thing as wanting him to be transparent. But Ajax's body is an obstacle to this, so during sex Sula fantasizes tearing off his skin, dissecting him layer by layer until she reaches the being beneath: rubbing his skin until the black disappears, taking a nail file or old paring knife to scrape at the layer of gold beneath, using a chisel to crack open what's left until the body is broken down to its earthly elements.[59] As she experiences this her body goes weak with a spreading orgasm: it ejects her from person-hood, swallowed by the violent unboundedness of sex.

Directly after this event Sula becomes the most conventional beribboned feminine lover imaginable: Ajax sees this, and he flees her; she declines and dies of a broken heart. Once again love's promise violently fails, and once again it is women who experience the impossibility of optimism (and of femininity) in the over-whelming face of its failure. Yet one might also say that *Sula* signals a different horizon of possibility for desire, a form of intimacy made of sights and smells and inchoate intensities, more than sounds, identity, or language: this form of desire disregards the conventional institutions and ideologies of intimacy, in-

---

[59] Toni Morrison, *Sula* (New York: Penguin, 1982), 130–31.

cluding conventional heterosexuality and the reproductive family, which seem in the book to ravage the very desires they uphold and societies they structure.

This desire for love to reach beyond the known world of law and language enables us to consider the idea that romantic love might sometimes serve as a placeholder for a less eloquent or institutionally proper longing. A love plot would, then, represent a desire for a life of unconflictedness, where the aggression inherent in intimacy is not lived as violence and submission to the discipline of institutional propriety or as the disavowals of true love, but as something less congealed into an identity or a promise, perhaps a mix of curiosity, attachment, and passion. But as long as the normative narrative and institutionalized forms of sexual life organize identity for people, these longings mainly get lived as a desire for love to obliterate the wildness of the unconscious, confirm the futurity of a known self, and dissolve the enigmas that marks one's lovers.

The formalism of Sula's desire, apparent throughout the novel, finds its most visible evidence in her will to destroy the object she loves in order to understand it. This opens up another way to address the logic of romantic love. If, on the one hand, the desire for transparency in love is associated with producing a deep internal calm about identity, on the other hand, desire frequently seeks out and occupies the extremes of feeling. Sula does not think she is having a violent fantasy about Ajax: she thinks that she is loving him, and that love means the emancipation from self, here figured in the materiality of his body. Yet Sula's desire to dissect her lover raises questions about the relation between romance and pornography: what if her fantasy were written as a man's desire for a woman, such that during sex, we read of the man's desire to slice away at the woman's body? What if this were a gay or queer fantasy, how would you read it then? Does an explanation that uses a paradigm of masculine sexual privilege to explain Sula's "confusion" of desire with fantasies of violence "solve" these questions of fantasy, power, ethics, otherness, and the effects of gendering?

Sharon Thompson and others argue that there is effectively no difference between pornographic representations of sex and romance conventions. Both of these are said to involve the overcoming of people by desires, and both fantasize scenes of sexuality using realist modes of representation. It has been suggested that women use romantic fantasy to experience the rush of these extremes the way men tend to use pornography, and that fantasizing about intensified feeling can be a way of imagining the thrill of sexual or political control or its loss, or, conversely, a way of overwhelming one's sexual ambivalence or insecurity with a frenzy of representation. It can also be a way of experiencing one's perverse impulses without taking on the identity "pervert." It is true that romance approaches the extremes of feeling and desire by way of a discourse of love: but love can be thought of as a way of managing the sheer ambiguity of romantic language and expectation. These suggestions give narrative shape to our previous discussion of the psychoanalytic model of fantasy. In that context, as well as here, these alternative possibilities for reading the sexual genres of fantasy express tensions internal to sexuality, and heterosexuality in particular. But insofar as heterosexuality has become the primary site that organizes self-knowledge and self-development, gay, lesbian and bisexual narratives of desire must be in dialogue with the utopian expectations of conventional love, and its different motives for fantasy.

I have been using fiction to give us a sense of love's narrative conventions. Fiction provides models of the relation between love's utopian prospects and its lived experience; and modern women's fiction in particular seeks to create subjects who identify with love's capacity to overcome the troubles of everyday life. This means that romantic narrative conventions argue for continuing to believe that femininity is defined through an unambivalent faith in the love plot while also developing a critical distance on that belief, as it measures the costs of women's submission to men (who are said to have less skill and investment in the project of intimacy).

This latter, critical, discourse has its own space outside of the novel: therapy culture. In the United States since the 1910s, love talk has been associated with therapeutic rhetoric in U.S. popular culture. Advice columns, self-help pedagogy, didactic short stories, moral exhortations, autobiographies, and case studies have popularized psychoanalysis, muted its discussions of the pervasiveness of perversion, and sought to help people, especially women, adjust their desires and their self-relations to the norms and forms of everyday life. (The gay and lesbian public sphere proliferates with self-help and advice literatures too: these scenes of representation and advice help non-normative sexual subjects trade information about the specificity of their practices of love and sex, which overlap without reproducing entirely the norms of heterosexual culture).

Self-help discourse has tended to reproduce the split in romance ideology that we have been developing: valorizing the promise of love and the mutual obligations of lovers, it presumes that problems in love must be solved by way of internal adjustment, to make certain that its conventional forms can remain and keep sustaining the signs of utopian intimacy. Individuals are told that: the normative ideologies and institutions of intimacy can work for them, but men and women are different species who will never experience the intimate other's desire in the same language or with the same intensity; there are "rules" of seduction and for the maintenance of the intimate other which should be followed, but about which it is bad to be explicit; romantic intimacy is an addiction that stimulates weakness and stunts growth, and yet is central to maturity; sex should be central, but not too central to love; the norms of propriety and responsibility that organize conventional lives are right, decent, and possible, but also boring, violent, and incomplete; and, within reason, anyone should get what she wants. This includes conventional norms about sexual practice itself: as discussions about sex have become more publicly available, it would seem that more varied practices have been normalized over the course of the twentieth century. Yet remaining remarkably stable has been the ideology that sex must seem natural: heterosexuality seems to require that any pedagogy between lovers must take place away from the sex itself, so that the image of the sex act as an expressive act of an unambivalent individual can be preserved. This form of hypocrisy is, currently, conventional to sex. Generally this ideology is addressed to women, who are deemed responsible for maintaining the emotional comfort of everyone in their sphere: but the unstated presumption in much self-help culture is that heterosexual intimacy is constantly in crisis and that its survival is crucial for the survival of life as we know it (a claim which is not false, but which of course does not tell the whole story of how desires are served by the reproduction of heterosexuality as a norm that gets called Nature).

When people whose sexual lives do not assimilate to the norms that are organized by this pedagogy adapt the logics of romantic love to themselves, they too can adapt their lives to the ways its institutions and moral codes have historically steadied and screened out the threatening instability of desire. But since, as we have suggested, gays and lesbians have had, historically, no institutions to enable the kinds of stability and disavowal available to heterosexuals, a greater degree of public explicitness has characterized non-normative forms of intimacy. This threatens traditional sexual subjects.[60] But these kinds of rhetorical and

---

[60] David Sedaris confirms this in the opening of his autobiographical tale, "ashes": "The moment I real-

practical improvisations on the "normal" life of lived desire does not mean that queer sexual subjects do not fantasize about love and its rich stabilizing promises the way straights do: the couple in love is a seductive desire, a fantasy of being emancipated into form's holding environment. But like all fantasies that might be lived, it requires a world that can sustain it, a context of law and norm that is only now emerging for gays and lesbians, just as it did not exist for women generally until the middle of the twentieth century.

Self-help consumers are exhorted to adjust themselves to these norms as though everyone, or at least all women, has the same, generic desires: and their failure to find a life to sustain their desires is the subject daily of interminable talk shows on television and radio, in gossip columns and fan magazines, on the Internet, and in the political public sphere. Yet that failure is not considered evidence of the impossibility of these theoretical statements about love: it is considered evidence of individual failure. As a result, an entire industry

---

ized I would be a homosexual for the rest of my life, I forced my brother and sisters to sign a contract swearing they'd never get married. There was a clause allowing them to live with anyone of their choice, just so long as they never made it official" (David Sedaris, *Naked* [Boston: Little, Brown, 1997], 235).

produces ever more therapeutic commodities offering strategies for surviving desire. Romance aesthetics is part of this strategy to link consumption to emotional survival. The huge industry of *things* that sustains itself on the reproduction of romantic fantasy (*Bridges*, for example, generated at least one film, two CDs, seven books, and reading groups worldwide) simultaneously de-isolates subjects who are suffering from desire, and yet names them as both the source of and the solution to their problems. (When was the last Marxist self-help book?) This emphasis pushes people to think of their private lives as the only material over which they might have any control (despite all the evidence to the contrary): as love and its intimate contexts come to bear the burden of establishing personal value generally, and especially for women, popular culture initiates a contradictory image set for establishing emancipatory agency. Love induces stuckness and freedom; love and its absences induce mental/emotional illness or *amour fou*; love is therapy for what ails you; love is the cause of what ails you. In that context, psychotherapy appears as that which can exacerbate or help you cure love sickness; popular culture genres offering wise conventionalities can cause and help you cure love sickness as well as or even better than psychotherapy.

Take, for example, the fantasy of romance as therapy that shapes the feminist "indie" art film, *Ruby Sparks* (Dayton and Farris, 2012). Calvin (Paul Dano), a pale, white male writer in the J.D. Salinger tradition of ficto-autobiography, has a massive writing block. He has no life, and he cannot write. His therapist suggests that, to cure his blockage both to fantasy and living, Calvin write about a person who can see what is lovable in his scruffy, drooly, gender-confused dog (a male dog that urinates in a bitch-squat style). Calvin does not find this suggestion comic or allegorical, which it is. Instead, he dreams about a young woman named Ruby Sparks giving that kind of kind attention to the abject dog, and then writes her into existence as his own lover to love and accept him completely. After being briefly disturbed about the psychotic implications of bringing his Real Doll to life (and unaware of the aesthetic precedents from Galatea on), he becomes a happy man living in a bubble with his ideal girl.

But as time passes, Calvin finds Ruby (Zoe Kazan) insufferable. He writes her as strong and artistic, but cannot tolerate her autonomy when she develops her own story; he rewrites her as a slavishly loving doormat, but is also turned off by her subordination when she turns to want only him. As he revises her according to the specifications of his wish, he both desires and loathes her, feeling in and out of control: does this mean that he is a bad writer, or an ordinary lover? He can't bear any revision, any version of *what he fantasizes that he wants*.

Finally, in a climatic, *Tales of Hoffman*-like scene, Calvin reveals Ruby to herself as an automaton, a non-human under his power. Then, converting from mad scientist/slave master to sentimental revolutionary, he writes a final page of the novel that ends it all, but not exactly by killing her — or himself. In his closing sentences he proclaims that "history" hereby releases Ruby to herself, and he delivers her unto "freedom." But this freedom from history and from Calvin's control turns out, in the end, to amount to *her amnesia about his control of her*. In contrast, while Calvin loses Ruby, he retains control over the memory of her. (See, in contrast, the similar plot of the 2004 Charlie Kaufman film *Eternal Sunshine of the Spotless Mind*, where the nebbish man and the dream-woman both erase their memories.)

As if to admit that she was nothing but a placeholder for his projections, Calvin then writes a successful "fiction" about this "real" woman, called, generically, *A Girlfriend,* which seems to be a hit. He then demands that his psychotherapist accept *his* fantasy of hetero-romance as real — that is, to accept that Ruby was flesh and blood real. This combination — to pretend to release control when he is exerting the most control; to demand that the judging world, in the person of his therapist, relinquish its control over the real to the patient's personal fantasy; and to then hold his control over everyone and everything as his enduring precious secret — is deemed a successful end of Calvin's therapy *and* the condition under which powerful art and love emerge.

Calvin's fantasy of an impossible love (whose structure is incoherent — contingent, contradictory, aggressive, passive, tender, and dissociated) occupies what Laplanche has called "a psychotic enclave." This separateness and misrecognition is just the condition of ordinary love, given the enabling structure of fantasy. What makes this particular film so revealing for our purposes is that popular therapeutic culture offers a form for seeming to repair the intractable fractures within and between people, by way of the demand for the very love that also intensifies these cleavages. But the film does not fall down once tied in these knots. Instead, in its habitation of the romantic comedy genre, the injuries of love are healed not by paying attention to the details of constancy and inconstancy love generates, and not by agreeing to try to live in love's awkward synchrony, but by insisting on the sovereignty of fantasy: accept *my* fantasy of love as *our* realism. This is like the conclusion that *Marnie* reached as well, but if in Hitchcock's film Marnie is the criminal/patient-as-lover who must accept Mark's fantasy or march off to prison, here the solution is deemed more just and satisfying for Ruby, because she has her "freedom" — from Calvin, memory, and consciousness.

What is the difference between Calvin's version of the lover's demand and a stalker's insistence that she is in a relationship with her unwilling object? The fantasy, which is at the heart both of popular culture and Lacanian psychoanalysis, is that love is the misrecognition you like, can bear, and will try to keep consenting to. If the Other will accept your fantasy/realism as the condition of their encounter with their own lovability, and if you will agree to accept theirs, the couple (it could be any relation) has a fighting chance not to be destroyed by the aggressive presence of ambivalence, with its jumble of memory, aggressive projection, and blind experimentation. This is not a cynical bargain, but the bargain that fantasy enables for any subject to take up a position in a sustained relation. At the same time, though, the film also calls on popular romance comedy genres to defang the violence and discomfort that inevitably ensue when the scene of love seeks out but never quite finds its resting form. The couple meets again in the film's final scene. When we meet Ruby at the beginning of the film, she is an unblocked painter who is untrained but has a lot of confidence in her art, and therefore she is all of the things that Calvin is not. At the end of the film, however, Ruby has no talent to distinguish herself. We encounter her lounging in the park, enjoying reading *A Girlfriend*, the book that is both her own story, and a story

that her amnesia bars her from recognizing as
hers. She asks Calvin not to ruin the ending; he
promises not to foretell and foreclose the
ending, this time. Their agreement, to keep a
secret and not to ask what it is, is the
foundation of their love. The secret is the secret
of their judgment of each other: but also he
knows a story she will now never know. To not
tell the ending is to not tell the beginning. It is
a "happy ending" for the film, as amnesia and
the closet are the conditions under which the
lovers will take up positions as mutual fan-
tasizers.

The film's attempt to use romance comedy
to heal the tragedy of what's unbearable in love
is predicted by its staging of their first real date
at a zombie movie, which is followed by a scene
where Calvin eats a dip that looks a lot like
brains. This joke about the conditions for
normative happiness sees the romance as more
likely to revitalize the zombie fantasy of heterosexual romance — to dip into it after it's dead
— than is the psychotherapy that Calvin under-
goes throughout the film. Psychotherapy
admits that fantasy is unconscious; popular
culture thinks it is all gesture, style, story, and
mood. If experience and memory dent love, it
argues, let's try to retain its new car smell by
foreclosing incidents that could become dis-
turbing events. So if popular culture does dip
into the scenarios of psychic fantasy that enable
the subject to bear the disturbed relation

between what Eve Sedgwick calls the reparative and destructive gestures of attachment to one's objects (persons and worlds), it also refuses any story that does not affirm love's fundamentally healing properties.

The use of the logic of romantic desire to neutralize, at least symbolically, the violence and attraction at play in hierarchical social relations implicitly suggests that structures and institutions of power can always be overcome by personal feelings, personal choices. It is not surprising, then, that the commodity form has a central place in the valorization of conventional or "normal" desire.[61] The interactions of capitalism and desire, as we have already seen, are extremely complicated and contested. Capitalism could not thrive without an attention to and constant stimulation of desire, which means that the centrality of romance and sex to its persuasive strategies creates subjects

---

[61] For histories of this relation see Eva Illouz, *Consuming the Romantic Utopia: Love and the Cultural Contradictions of Capitalism* (Berkeley: University of California Press, 1997) and Kathy Lee Peiss, *Cheap Amusements: Working Women in Turn-of-the-Century New York* (Philadelphia: Temple University Press, 1986).

simultaneously primed for conventional intimacy and profit-generating relations to consumption and labor.

Marx classically notes that the magical autonomy of the commodity form obscures the economic, social, and ideological relations that animate it in the process of its production: so, too, the mass cultural discourse of romance obscures, the way a fetish does, the relations between the hegemonic processes of collective life and what people typically imagine as love. People learn to identify with love the way they identify with commodities: the notions of personal autonomy, consent, choice, and fulfillment so powerful in love discourse seem to be the same as those promised by national capitalism. At the same time, romance is a vehicle for marketing heterosexuality as the very form of fantasy and also the normal context in which fantasy can be lived, but not in a generic way: the heteronormative love plot is at its most ideological when it produces subjects who believe that their love story expresses their true, nuanced, and unique feelings, their own personal destiny.

This idealistic and commodified aspect of romance has also inspired some ways of relating dominant and subordinate peoples to each other across fields of difference and ambivalence. As we described earlier, liberal political culture posits individual autonomy and self-development at the center of value in social life. Romance ideology participates in this project by depicting sentiment or *feeling* as the essential and universal truth of persons. Feeling is what people have in common despite their apparent differences. Thus liberals have long responded to antagonism between dominant and subordinate peoples by saying to the dominant culture: the people you think of as Other only *appear* to threaten your stability and value by their difference; they have feelings too; they suffer too; therefore you are essentially alike. You desire the same thing "they" do, to feel unconflicted, to have intimacy. If you feel ambivalent, or in some relation of antagonism and fascination to the members of the population from which you feel intensely estranged, you can understand your unease the way you understand sexual difference under heterosexuality, as something that can be overcome by *desire* and cultivated *identification*. Many people argue that love of the other is a powerful tool for bringing marginalized groups into the dominant social world; on the other hand, sentimental identification with suffering created by national, racial, economic, and religious privilege has long coexisted with laws that discriminate among particular forms of difference, privileging some against others (see laws against interracial, interreligious, or gay marriage, for instance).

CONCLUSION

What are the relations among the world-building drives of love, the critical and utopian fantasies contained there, the project of psychoanalysis (the science), and self-help (its popular culture)? How does the constant return of the subject to adjusting herself and her intimate others at the scene of her conflicted desire enable and disable the difficult and risky parts of self- and social transformation? What is the relation between the aggressivity of desire and its need to protect and sustain its objects despite also exposing them to fantasy's projections, negations, idealizations — distortions? Apart from creating jealousy, threat, or moral superiority, what might it do to people to reveal to themselves and each other that their particular desires are unbearable in their contradictions, unknown in their potential contours, and yet demand reliable and confirming recognitions? How might it become bearable to face the ways visceral responses combine convention and something else, perhaps inarticulate or illegitimate desires? What does it mean that, unreliable in desire, we nonetheless demand the other to be perfectly attuned to what's out of tune? Where are the social infrastructures through which people can reimagine their relation to intimacy and the life building organized around it in ways that are as yet uninevitable or unimaginable?

This little book has tried to say some things about desire and love: that there are no master explanations of them; that they destabilize and threaten the very things (like identity and life) that they are disciplined to organize and ameliorate; that there is a long history of using the abstractions and institutions of "love" as signs and sites of propriety, so that the "generic" subjects imagined in a love plot tend to be white, Western, heterosexual, and schooled to the protocols of "bourgeois" privacy; that these tacit proprieties have been used to justify the economic and physical domination of nations, races, religions, gays, lesbians, and women. Yet here the story must return to the happy ending in which desire melds with the love that speaks its conventional name. Even now, despite everything, desire/love continues to exert a utopian promise to discover a form that is elastic enough to manage what living throws at lovers. In telling the story of some things that have been touched by the intensities of desire, fantasy, and love, the project of this book is also to reopen the utopian to more promises than have yet been imagined and sustained.

REFERENCES

Abel, Elizabeth, Barbara Christian, and Helene Moglen, eds. 1997. *Female Subjects in Black and White: Race, Psychoanalysis, Feminism*. Berkeley: University of California Press.

Aronowitz, Stanley. 1984. "When the Left was New." In *The 60s Without Apology*, eds. Sohnya Sayers, Anders Stephanson, Stanley Aronowitz, and Fredric Jameson, special issue of *Social Text* 9/10 (1984): 11–43.

Apter, Emily and William Pietz, eds. 1993. *Fetishism as Cultural Discourse*. Ithaca: Cornell University Press.

Barthes, Roland. 1975. *The Pleasure of the Text*, trans. Richard Miller. New York: Hill and Wang.

Barthes, Roland. 1976. *Sade, Fourier, Loyola*, trans. Richard Miller. New York: Hill and Wang.

Benjamin, Jessica. 1995. *Like Subjects, Love Objects: Essays on Recognition and Sexual Difference*. New Haven: Yale University Press.

Berger, John. 1972. *Ways of Seeing*. London: Penguin Books.

Berlant, Lauren. 1994. "'68, or Something." *Critical Inquiry* 21 (Autumn): 124–55.

Berlant, Lauren. 1997. *The Queen of America Goes to Washington City: Essays on Sex and Citizenship*. Durham: Duke University Press.

Berlant, Lauren. 1998. "Intimacy: A Special Issue." *Critical Inquiry* 24: 281–88.

Berlant, Lauren and Michael Warner. 1998. "Sex in Public." *Critical Inquiry* 24: 547–66.

Bersani, Leo. 1986. *The Freudian Body: Psychoanalysis and Art*. New York: Columbia University Press.

Bersani, Leo and Adam Phillips. 2008. *Intimacies*. Chicago: University of Chicago Press.

Brennan, Teresa. 1992. *The Interpretation of the Flesh: Freud and Femininity*. London: Routledge.

Brennan, Teresa. 1993. *History after Lacan.* London: Routledge.

Burger, Glenn. 2003. *Chaucer's Queer Nation.* Minneapolis: University of Minnesota Press.

Burgin, Victor. 1996. *In/different Spaces: Place and Memory in Visual Culture* Berkeley: University of California Press.

Butler, Judith P. 1990. *Gender Trouble: Feminism and the Subversion of Identity.* New York: Routledge.

Butler, Judith P. 1993. *Bodies that Matter.* New York: Routledge.

Chatterjee, Partha. 1994. *The Nation and its Fragments: Colonial and Postcolonial Histories.* New York: Oxford University Press.

Chauncey, George. 1994. *Gay New York: Gender, Urban Culture, and the Makings of the Gay Male World, 1890-1940.* New York: Basic Books.

Chodorow, Nancy. 1978. *The Reproduction of Mothering: Psychoanalysis and the Sociology of Gender.* Berkeley: University of California Press.

Cixous, Hélène. 1976. "The Laugh of the Medusa," trans. Keith Cohen and Paula Cohen. *Signs* 1.4: 875–93

Cixous, Hélène. [1976] 1983. "Portrait of Dora," trans. Sarah Burd. *Diacritics* 13.1: 2–32.

Copjec, Joan. 1994. *Read My Desire: Lacan Against the Historicists*. Cambridge, Mass.: MIT Press.

D'Emilio, John and Estelle B. Freedman. 1988. *Intimate Matters: A History of Sexuality in America*. New York: Harper and Row.

De Lauretis, Teresa. 1994. *The Practice of Love: Lesbian Sexuality and Perverse Desire*. Bloomington: Indiana University Press.

Deleuze, Gilles. 1971. *Masochism: An Interpretation of Coldness and Cruelty*, trans. Jean McNeil. New York: George Braziller.

Deleuze, Gilles. 1992. "Postscript on the Societies of Control." *October* 59: 3–7.

Deleuze, Gilles and Félix Guattari. 1977. *Anti-Oedipus: Capitalism and Schizophrenia*, trans. Robert Hurley, Mark Seem, and Helen R. Lane. New York: Viking Press.

Doane, Mary Ann. 1991. *Femmes Fatales: Feminism, Film Theory, Psychoanalysis*. New York: Routledge.

Echols, Alice. 1989. *Daring to Be Bad: Radical Feminism in America, 1967-1975*. Minneapolis: University of Minnesota Press.

Edelman, Lee. 1993. *Homographesis: Essays in Gay Literary and Cultural Theory*. New York: Routledge.

Faderman, Lillian. 1991. *Odd Girls and Twilight Lovers: A History of Lesbian Life in Twentieth Century America*. New York: Columbia University Press.

Fradenburg, L.O. Aranye. *Sacrifice Your Love: Psychoanalysis, Historicism, Chaucer*. Minneapolis: University of Minnesota Press, 2002.

Fradenburg, Louise and Carla Freccero, eds. *Premodern Sexualities*. 1996. New York: Routledge.

Freud, Sigmund. [1905] 1949. *Three Essays on the Theory of Sexuality*. In *The Standard Edition of the Complete Psychological Works of Sigmund Freud*, trans. and ed. James Strachey. Vol. 7. London: Hogarth Press.

Freud, Sigmund. [1923] 1961. "The Ego and the Id." In *The Standard Edition of the Complete Psychological Works of Sigmund Freud*, trans. and ed. James Strachey. Vol. 19. London: Hogarth Press.

Freud, Sigmund. [1924] 1957. "The Economic Problem of Masochism." In *The Standard Edition of the Complete Psychological Works of Sigmund Freud*, trans. and ed. James Strachey. Vol. 12. London: Hogarth Press.

Freud, Sigmund. [1925] 1961. "Some Psychical Consequences of the Anatomical Distinction Between the Sexes." In *The Standard Edition of the Complete Psychological Works of Sigmund Freud*, trans. and ed. James Strachey. Vol. 19. London: Hogarth Press.

Freud, Sigmund. [1933] 1964. "Femininity." In *New Introductory Essays on Psychoanalysis*, in *The Standard Edition of the Complete Psychological Works of Sigmund Freud*, trans. and ed. James Strachey. Vol. 22. London: Hogarth Press. 136–57.

Gallop, Jane. 1982. *The Daughter's Seduction: Feminism and Psychoanalysis*. Ithaca: Cornell University Press.

Gilman, Sander. 1985. *Difference and Pathology: Stereotypes of Sexuality, Race, and Madness*. Ithaca: Cornell University Press.

Goldberg, Jonathan and Madhavi Menon. 2005. "Queering History." *PMLA* 120.5: 1608–617.

Griggers, Camilla. 1997. *Becoming-Woman*. Minneapolis: University of Minnesota Press.

Grosz, Elizabeth A. 1994. *Volatile Bodies: Toward a Corporeal Feminism*. Bloomington: Indiana University Press.

Halley, Janet. 1995. "The Politics of the Closet: Legal Articulation of Sexual Orientation Identity." In *After Identity: A Reader in Law and Culture*, eds. Dan Daniels and Karen Engle. New York: Routledge. 24–38.

Halperin, David. 2002. *How to Do the History of Homosexuality*. Chicago: University of Chicago Press.

Haraway, Donna. 1991. *Simians, Cyborgs, and Women*. New York: Routledge.

Herdt, Gilbert H. 1997. *Same Sex, Different Cultures: Gays and Lesbians Across Cultures*. Boulder: Westview Press.

Illouz, Eva. 1997. *Consuming the Romantic Utopia: Love and the Cultural Contradictions of Capitalism*. Berkeley: University of California Press.

Irigaray, Luce. 1985. *Speculum of the Other Woman*, translated by Gillian Gill. Ithaca: Cornell University Press.

Jameson, Fredric. 1979. "Reification and Utopia in Mass Culture." *Social Text* 1: 130–48.

Kaplan, Caren. 1996. *Questions of Travel: Postmodern Discourses of Displacement*. Durham: Duke University Press.

Kaplan, Cora. 1986. "*The Thorn Birds*: Fiction, Fantasy, Femininity." In *Formations of Fantasy*, eds. Victor Burgin, James Donald, and Cora Kaplan. London: Methuen. 142–66.

Katz, Jonathan Ned. 1995. *The Invention of Heterosexuality*. New York: Dutton.

Kennedy, Elizabeth Lapovsky and Madeline Davis. 1993. *Boots of Leather, Slippers of Gold: The History of a Lesbian Community*. New York: Routledge.

Klein, Melanie and Joan Rivière. 1964. *Love, Hate, and Reparation*. New York: Norton.

Kristeva, Julia. 1980. *Desire in Language*. New York: Columbia University Press.

Kristeva, Julia. [1980] 1982. *Powers of Horror: Essays in Abjection*, trans. Leon S. Roudiez. New York: Columbia University Press.

Lacan, Jacques. 1977. *Ecrits*, trans. Alan Sheridan. New York: W.W. Norton.

Lacan, Jacques. 1982. *Feminine Sexuality: Jacques Lacan and the École Freudienne*, eds. Jacqueline Rose and Juliet Mitchell. New York: W.W. Norton.

Laplanche, Jean. 1976. *Life and Death in Psychoanalysis*, trans. Jeffrey Mehlman. Baltimore: Johns Hopkins University Press. 17–21.

Laplanche, Jean and J.-B. Pontalis. 1973. *The Language of Psycho-Analysis*, trans. Donald Nicholson-Smith. London: Hogarth Press.

Laplanche, Jean and J.-B. Pontalis. [1964] 1986. "Fantasy and the Origins of Sexuality." In *Formations of Fantasy*, eds. Burgin, Donald, and Kaplan. 5–34.

Lipsitz, George. 1990. *Time Passages*. Minneapolis: University of Minnesota Press.

Lochrie, Karma. 2005. *Heterosyncracies: Female Sexuality When Normal Wasn't*. Minneapolis: University of Minnesota Press.

Lochrie, Karma, Peggy McCracken, and James Schultz, eds. 1997. *Constructing Medieval Sexuality*. Minneapolis: University of Minnesota Press.

Marcuse, Herbert. 1964. *One-Dimensional Man*. Boston: Beacon Books.

Marcuse, Herbert. 1969. *An Essay on Liberation*. Boston: Beacon Books.

McClintock, Ann. 1995. *Imperial Leather: Race, Gender, and Sexuality in the Colonial Contest*. New York: Routledge.

Minsky, Rosalind, ed. 1996. *Psychoanalysis and Gender: An Introductory Reader*. New York: Routledge.

Mitchell, Juliet. 1974. *Psychoanalysis and Feminism*. New York: Random House.

Modleski, Tania. 1982. *Loving with a Vengeance: Mass-Produced Fantasies for Women*. Hamden: Archon Books.

Morrison, Toni. [1973] 1982. *Sula*. New York: Penguin.

Mulvey, Laura. [1975] 1989. "Visual Pleasure and Narrative Cinema." In *Visual and Other Pleasures.* Bloomington: Indiana University Press. 14–29.

Negt, Oskar and Alexander Kluge. 1993. *Public Sphere and Experience: Toward an Analysis of the Bourgeois and Proletarian Public Sphere.* Minneapolis: University of Minnesota Press.

Newton, Esther. 1995. *Cherry Grove Fire Island: Sixty Years in America's First Gay and Lesbian Town.* Boston: Beacon Press.

Peiss, Kathy Lee. 1986. *Cheap Amusements: Working Women in Turn-of-the-Century New York.* Philadelphia: Temple University Press.

Phillips, Adam. 1994. "Freud and the Uses of Forgetting." In *On Flirtation: Psychoanalytic Essays on the Uncommitted Life.* London: Faber and Faber. 22-38.

Probyn, Elspeth. 1996. *Outside Belongings.* New York: Routledge.

Rabine, Leslie W. 1985. "Romance in the Age of Electronics: Harlequin Enterprises." In *Feminist Criticism and Social Change: Sex, Class and Race in Literature and Culture,* eds. Judith Newton and Deborah Rosenfelt. New York: Methuen. 249–67.

Radway, Janice A. 1984. *Reading the Romance: Women, Patriarchy, and Popular Literature.* Chapel Hill: University of North Carolina Press.

Roof, Judith. 1991. *A Lure of Knowledge: Lesbian Sexuality and Theory.* New York: Columbia University Press.

Rose, Jacqueline. 1986. *Sexuality in the Field of Vision.* London: Verso.

Rose, Jacqueline. 1982. "Introduction II." In *Feminine Sexuality: Jacques Lacan and the École Freudienne*, eds. Jaqueline Rose and Juliet Mitchell. New York: W.W. Norton. 27–57.

Sayers, Sohnya, Anders Stephanson, Stanley Aronowitz, and Fredric Jameson, eds. 1984. *The 60s Without Apology.* Special Issue of *Social Text* 9/10.

Saunders, Jean. 1995. *The Craft of Writing Romance.* London: Allison and Busby.

Schor, Naomi. 1987. *Reading in Detail: Aesthetics and the Feminine.* New York: Methuen.

Schor, Naomi. 1985. "Female Fetishism: The Case of Georges Sand." *Poetics Today* 6: 301–10.

Schor, Naomi. 1993. "Fetishism and Its Ironies." In Apter and Pietz, edss, *Fetishism as Cultural Discourse*. 92–100.

Sedaris, David. 1997. *Naked*. Boston: Little, Brown and Co.

Sedgwick, Eve Kosofsky. 1993. "A Poem is Being Written." In *Tendencies*. Durham: Duke University Press. 206–11.

Sedgwick, Eve Kosofsky. 1990. *Epistemology of the Closet*. Berkeley: University of California Press.

Silverman, Kaja. 1988. *The Acoustic Mirror: The Female Voice in Psychoanalysis and Cinema*. Bloomington: Indiana University Press.

Snitow, Ann, Christine Stansell, and Sharon Thompson. 1983. *Powers of Desire: the Politics of Sexuality*. New York: Monthly Review Press.

Sommer, Doris. 1984. *Foundational Fictions: The National Romances of Latin America*. Berkeley: University of California Press, 1984.

Spillers, Hortense J. 1987. "Mama's Baby, Papa's Maybe: An American Grammar Book." *Diacritics* 17: 64–81.

Spivak, Gayatri Chakravorty. 1992. "Acting Bits/Identity Talk." *Critical Inquiry* 18: 770–803.

Steedman, Carolyn Kay. 1986. *Landscape for a Good Woman: A Story of Two Lives*. New Brunswick: Rutgers University Press.

Taylor, Helen. 1989. *Scarlett's Women: Gone with the Wind and its Female Fans*. New Brunswick: Rutgers University Press.

Thompson, Sharon. 1995. *Going All the Way: Teenage Girls' Tales of Sex, Romance, and Pregnancy*. New York: Hill and Wang.

Viego, Antonio. 2007. *Dead Subjects: Toward a Politics of Loss in Latino Studies*. Durham: Duke University Press.

Waller, Robert James. 1992. *The Bridges of Madison County*. New York: Warner Books.

Warner, Michael. 1993. *Fear of a Queer Planet: Queer Politics and Social Theory*. Minneapolis: University of Minnesota Press.

Willis, Ellen, 1984. "Radical Feminism and Feminist Radicalism." In *The 60s Without Apology*, eds. Sayres, Stephanson, Aronowitz, and Jameson. 91–118.

Winnicott, D.W. 1958. *Collected Papers: Through Paediatrics to Psychoanalysis*. London: Hogarth Press.

Winnicott, D.W. 1971. *Playing and Reality*. London: Routledge.

Winnicott, D.W. 1986. *Home is Where We Start From: Essays by a Psychoanalyist*. New York: W.W. Norton.

Wittig, Monique. 1992. *The Straight Mind and Other Essays*. Boston: Beacon Press.

Žižek, Slavoj. 1989. *The Sublime Object of Ideology*. London: Verso.

Žižek, Slavoj. 1994. *The Metastases of Enjoyment: Six Essays on Woman and Causality*. London: Verso.

Žižek, Slavoj. 1994a. "The Spectre of Ideology." In *Mapping Ideology*, ed. Slavoj Žižek. London: Verso. 1-33.

W. dreams, like Phaedrus, of an army of thinker-friends, thinker-lovers. He dreams of a thought-army, a thought-pack, which would storm the philosophical Houses of Parliament. He dreams of Tartars from the philosophical steppes, of thought-barbarians, thought-outsiders. What distances would shine in their eyes!

~Lars Iyer

www.babelworkinggroup.org

Made in United States
North Haven, CT
03 July 2023

38516972R10078